A HISTORY OF COLOR

A HISTORY OF COLOR

Stanley Moss

New and Collected Poems

Seven Stories Press

New York

Seven Stories Press
140 Watts Street
New York, NY 10013
http://www.sevenstories.com

In Canada:
Hushion House, 36 Northline Road, Toronto, Ontario M4B 3E2

In the U.K.:
Turnaround Publisher Services Ltd., Unit 3, Olympia Trading Estate, Coburg Road, Wood Green, London N22 6TZ

In Australia:
Palgrave Macmillan, 627 Chapel Street, South Yarra VIC 3141

Library of Congress Cataloging-in-Publication Data

Moss, Stanley.
  A history of color : new and collected poems / Stanley Moss.-- 1st ed.
    p. cm.
  ISBN 1-58322-485-8 (pbk.)
  I. Title.
PS3563.O885H57 2003
811'.54--dc21
                                        2003005715
9 8 7 6 5 4 3 2 1

College professors may order examination copies of Seven Stories Press titles free for a six-month trial period. To order, visit www.sevenstories.com/textbook, or fax on school letterhead to (212) 226-1411.

Printed in Canada

God is the sole being who has no need to exist in order to reign.

BAUDELAIRE

ACKNOWLEDGMENTS

The American Poetry Review, The New Yorker, Poetry Nation (UK), *Poetry, The Times Literary Supplement, Poetry London, The New York Times, The Nation, Partisan Review, Pequod, Parnassus, Best American Poems of 2003, Shirim, The New Republic, The Forward, Dissent, Exile, Tikkun, The Virginia Quarterly, The Kentucky Review, Verse, Exquisite Corpse, Poetry International, Princeton University Library Chronicle*

FOR JANE AND TOBIA

AUTHOR'S NOTE

These poems are collected very roughly in reverse chronological order. Owing to late additions and revisions, several of the poems fall out of place; these are dated. A number of poems from early collections have been reworked. I am certain no reader will miss the early versions.

CONTENTS

II. Poems from ASLEEP IN THE GARDEN (1997) and
    THE INTELLIGENCE OF CLOUDS (1989)

III. Poems from SKULL OF ADAM (1979) and
    THE WRONG ANGEL (1966)

1
A History of Color

A HISTORY OF COLOR

1.

What is heaven but the history of color,
dyes washed out of laundry, cloth and cloud,
mystical rouge, lipstick, eye shadows? Harlot nature,
explain the color of tongue, lips, nipples,
against Death come ons of labia, penis, the anus,
the concupiscent color wheels of insects and birds,
explain why Christian gold and blue tempt the kneeling,
why Moslem green is miraculous in the desert,
why the personification of the rainbow is Iris,
the mother of Eros, why *Adam* in Hebrew
comes out of the redness of earth. . .
The cosmos and impatiens I planted this June
may outlast me, these yellow, pink and blue annuals
do not sell indulgences, a rose ravishes a rose.
The silver and purple pollen that has blown on the roof
of my car concludes a sacred conversation.

Against Death washerwomen and philosophers
sought a fixative for colors to replace unstable substances
like saliva, urine and blood, the long process of boiling
washing and rinsing. It is Death who works
with clean hands and a pure heart. Against him
Phoenician red-purple dyes taken from sea snails, the colors
fixed by exposing wool to air of the morning seas near Sidon,
or the sunlight and winds on the limestone cliffs of Crete—
all lost, which explains a limestone coastline
changed into mountains of pink-veined marble,
the discarded bodies of gods.
Of course Phoenician purple made for gods

and heroes cannot be produced nowadays.
Virgil thought purple was the color of the soul—
all lost. Anyone can see the arithmetic when purple
was pegged to the quantity and price of seashells.

Remember
the common gray and white seagull looked down
at the Roman Republic, at the brick-red and terra-cotta
dominant after the pale yellow stone of the Greek world,
into the glare of the Empire's white marble.
The sapphire and onyx housefly that circled
the jeweled crowns of Byzantium buzzed prayers,
thinks what it thinks, survives. Under a Greek sky
the churches held Christ alive to supplicants,
a dove alighted on a hand torn by nails.
In holy light and darkness
the presence of Christ is cupped in silver.
Death holds, whether you believe Christ
is there before you or not, you will not see Him later—
sooner prick the night sky with a needle to find the moon.

2.

I fight Death with peppermints, a sweet to recall
the Dark Ages before the word *orange* existed.
In illuminated manuscripts St. Jerome,
his robes *egg-red*, is seen translating in the desert,
a golden lion at his feet—
or he is tied to a column naked in a dream,
flagellated for reading satires and Pliny's
Natural History that describes
the colors used by Apelles, the Greek master,
in a painting of grapes so true to life
birds would alight on them to feed.
Death, you tourist, you've seen it all and better before,

4

your taste: whipped saints sucking chastity's thumb,
while you eat your candy of diseased and undernourished infants.

On an afternoon when death seemed no more than a newspaper
in a language I could not read, I remember
looking down at Jerusalem from the Mount of Olives,
that my friend said: "Jerusalem is a harlot,
everyone who passes leaves a gift."
Do birds of prey sing madrigals?
Outside the walls of Jerusalem, the crusaders
dumped mounts of dead Muslims
and their green banners, the severed heads of Jews,
some still wrapped in prayer shawls,
while the Christian dead sprawled near the place of a skull
which is called in Hebrew *Golgotha.*
Among the living, blood and blood-soaked prayers,
on the land of God's broken promises—a flagged javelin
stuck into the Holy Sepulcher as into a wild boar.

Hauled back by the *Franks*, colors never seen in Europe,
wonders of Islam, taffetas, organdies, brocades, damasks.
Gold-threaded cloth that seemed made for the Queen of Heaven
was copied in Italy on certain paintings of Our Lady,
on her blue robes in gold in Arabic:
"There is no God but God, Muhammad is His Prophet"—
for whom but Death to read?
Wrapped in a looted prayer rug,
an idea seized by Aquinas: the separation of faith and reason.
Later nicked from the library of Baghdad:
the invention of paper brought from China
by pilgrims on a hajj, looted rhyme, lenses,
notes on removing cataracts.
Certain veils would be lifted from the eyes of Europe,
all only for Death to see.

Within sight of Giotto's white, green and pink marble bell-tower
that sounded the promise of Paradise,
plants and insects were used for dyes made from oak gall,
bastard saffron, beetle, canary weed, cockroach,
the fixative was fermented piss from a young boy
or a man drunk on red wine, while the painters
mixed their pigments with egg yolks and albumen,
gold with lime, garlic, wax and casein
that dried hard as adamantine, buffed with a polished agate
or a wolf's tooth.

At the time of the Plague, while the dead
lay unattended in the streets of Europe,
the yellow flag hung out more often than washing,
someone cloistered wrote a text
on making red from cinnabar, saffron from crocus,
each page an illuminated example.
At the Last Supper the disciples sat dead at table.
Still, by the late fifteenth century
color was seen as ornament,
almost parallel to the colors of rhetoric,
blue was moving away from its place describing
the vaults of heaven to the changing sky of everyday.
Does it matter to heaven if a sleeve is blue or red or black?
In Venice Titian found adding lead-white to azurite-blue
changed a blue sleeve to satin.

3.

I think the absence of color is like a life without love.
A master can draw every passion with a pencil, but light,
shadow and dark cannot reveal the lavender Iris
between the opened thighs of a girl still almost a child,
or, before life was through with her, the red and purple
pomegranate at the center of her being.

Against Death on an English day Newton discovered
a single ray of white light refracted,
decomposed into a spectrum of colors,
and that he could reconstruct the totality,
mischievously reverse the process,
then produce white light again—which perhaps is why
last century, in a painting by Max Ernst,
the Holy Mother is spanking the baby Jesus.

Goethe found a like proof on a sunny summer day—
the birds, I suppose, as usual devouring insects
courting to the last moment of life.
While sitting by a crystal pool watching
soldiers fishing for trout, the poet was taken
by spectrums of color refracted from a ceramic shard
at the bottom of the pool, then from the tails of swimming trout
catching fire and disappearing,
until a rush of thirsty horses, tired and dirtied by war,
muddied the waters.

A heroic tenor sings to the exploding sun:
"Every war is a new dawning"—Fascist music.
Death would etch Saturn devouring his children on coins,
if someone would take his money.
Of course his I O U is good as gold.

Turner had sailors lash him to the mast
to see into a storm, then he painted slavers
throwing overboard the dead and dying,
sharks swimming through shades of red.
Later he painted the atheist Avalanche, then heaven
in truthful colors: Rain, Steam, Speed.
"Portraits of nothing and very like," they said, "tinted steam."
Turner kept most of his paintings to leave to England,
his Burning of the Houses of Parliament.

Against oblivion a still life of two red apples
stands for a beautiful woman. On her shoulder
the bruise of a painter's brush—she is no more
than a still life of peasant shoes.
"You will not keep apples or shoes or France," Death says.
A child chooses an object first for color,
then for form, in rooms with mother, father,
Death, and all the relatives of being.

4.

Now this coloratura moves off-stage
to the present, which is a kind of intermission.
My friend Mark Rothko painted a last canvas,
gray and yellow, then took a kitchen knife, half cut off his wrists
bound and knotted behind his back,
(a trick of the mind Houdini never mastered),
to throw off Eros, who rode his back and whipped him
even after he was dead, till Eros, the little Greek,
was covered with blood of the Song of Songs.
Now Rothko is a study of color, a purple chapel,
a still river where he looks for his mother and father.

Death, you tourist with too much luggage,
you can distinguish the living from your dead.
Can you tell Poseidon's trident from a cake fork,
the living from the living,
winter from summer, autumn from spring?
In a sunless world, even bats nurse their young,
hang upside down looking for heaven,
make love in a world where the lion, afraid of no beast,
runs in terror from a white chicken. Such are your winnings.
Death, I think you take your greatest pleasure

in watching us murdering in great numbers
in ways even you have not planned.
They say in paradise every third thought is of earth
and a woman with a child at her breast.

TO MY FRIEND BORN BLIND

You told me your blindness is not seeing
even the shades of black called darkness.
You felt useless as a mirror until you made a poem
useful as a dog with bells around its neck.
Sometimes you wake to the wind moving through different trees.
A child, you loved to touch your mother's face,
you wished the world were ocean,
you could hear, smell, and taste knew that it was blue.
Trees had a smell you called green, apples red.
How could the flag be red-white-and-blue?
You laugh when I tell you "drink to me only with thine eyes"
is a love song, that some who see
only make love in the dark. You wish you could see as a bat.
Mozart you say is the great equalizer, the truest democrat,
you always preferred a dog to a cane.
When in Braille you first read, "the disciples asked,
'Rabbi, who sinned this man or his parents that he was born blind?'
Jesus answering, 'Neither hath this man sinned nor his parents,
but that the works of God should be revealed in him...'
and he spat on the ground and healed the man
with his spit and mud—" you waited awhile, then read on.
Blind in dreams, you touch, taste, smell and hear—
see nothing, nightmares like crowds are the more terrible
because you never see what terrifies you.
Since childhood it was an act of faith
to believe the sun and moon were in the sky,
it pleased you the sun is a fire the sighted cannot look into...
It is late. As always you, my imaginary friend,
take me by the hand and lead me to bed.

SUBWAY TOKEN

If Walt Whitman were alive and young and still living in Brooklyn,
he would have seen the burning Trade Center,
and if he were old and still in Camden, New Jersey,
he would have seen men jumping out from a hundred stories up,
some holding hands, believers and nonbelievers
who prefer a leap of faith to a death in an ocean of fire.
Walt could have seen women falling from the sun,
although the sun has no offices.
True in the heavens there often has been a kind of tit for tat,
not just thunder for lightning:
where there is grandeur observed, something human, trivial.

The South Tower fell like the old Whitman,
although it was second to be struck,
then the North Tower like the young Whitman.
What history, what hallucination?
Anyone could see the towers fell like the great poet,
with three thousand people from eighty-seven countries,
and three hundred and forty-three firefighters
into the irrational fires that burned for ninety days.
None of these persons lived in boarding houses
as would be likely in Whitman's time.
History, hallucination?
A life goes up in flame like a page of bible paper.
You could not pile books so high, not good books,
as this grand canyon of steel and concrete body parts,
my city's broken backbone pushed out through his throat.

THE BLANKET

The man who never prays
accepts that the wheat field in summer
kneels in prayer when the wind blows across it,
that the wordless rain and snow
protect the world from blasphemy.
His wife covers him with a blanket
on a cold night—it is, perhaps, a prayer?
The man who never prays says kindness and prayer
are close, but not as close as sleep and death.
He does not observe the Days of Awe,
all days are equally holy to him.
In late September, he goes swimming
in the ocean, surrounded by divine intervention.

THE LOUSE

In a room overlooking Jerusalem,
I felt something like a leaf on my forehead—
I picked off a louse,
squashed it between the labyrinths
of my index finger and my thumb.
I have faith every louse in Jerusalem
has come through hair and feather:
Jew, Moslem, Christian
from wing to head to beard to crotch,
from cat's ear to rat's balls...
At the Jerusalem wall between Heaven and Hell
the unprepared are given skull-caps—
I refused a clean, gray paper cap,
the kind given children in different colors
at birthday parties with other favors;
I picked dusty black rayon someone left behind,
despite my friend's warning: "You may get lice."
Whatever the time of day, a little before fear,
the sun hurt my eyes. I kissed the wall
but had nothing further to say to it...
My louse's cousins have spent time among hyena packs,
nestled in carrion, under pus, lip to lip with maggots.
Surely Christ, who suffered crucifixion,
felt the bite of a louse. My fingers are Roman soldiers
if the louse I squashed had a trace of Christ's blood.
I have faith King David after all his adventures
had an itch in the groin, and a louse danced with him.
Once a winged horse with a peacock's tail
and a woman's face flew into this city from Arabia
with a prophet on its back.
We all can use a little sacred preening and combing.
I should be grateful for another louse.

THE FALCON

My son carries my ghost on his shoulder, a falcon,
I am careful not to dig in my claws. I play
I am his father owl, sometimes sparrow, a hummingbird
in his ear. I told him from my first chirp:
"Be an American democratic Jew mensch-bird."
When he was a child in Italy I was a migrant bird
with a nest in America. When I flew home
he cried *"Perche, perche?"* I wept
not wanting him to have a distant bird
or a sea captain for a father.
How many times did I cross the Atlantic
in the worst weather to perch outside his window?
What kind of nest could I make in Italy
on a hotel balcony? When he needed to be held
his mother and nannies held him. When he reached out
to me he often fell. He said *I know I know* to everything
I might have taught him. I fought for his life
with one wing tied behind my back—
for his name, school, and to have his hair cut
in a man's barber shop, not a salon for signoras.
"Lose to him! Lose to him!" his mother screamed.
I was the only one in his life
who would not throw a footrace
he could win in a year, fair and square.
How could a small boy spend so much time
laughing and talking to a father in restaurants?
He complained in Bologna I took him to six museums,
in Florence four, in Espagna mille e tre.
We laughed at those rare Italian birds
who don't find themselves sleeping forever
on a bed of polenta—preening, displaying,

making a bella figura. An omen in his life.
I flew him to an English meadow
to study Dante, then Shakespeare's histories
in a king maple overlooking the Hudson,
the cast: himself, me, my mate the beautiful Jane bird.

What are years? Not a herd of cattle,
perhaps a flock of birds passing overhead.
Sometimes I hear him chirping my song
louder than I ever sang it.
One day, when the heavenly dogs and hell dogs
find me behind a bush and fight over me,
may one with a soft mouth break from the pack
and take most of me to his Master. Let Him say, "Good dog,
good dog, what a peculiar kind of bird is this,
with his gray curly feathers and strange beak?
Have I ever heard him sing?" May it dawn upon Him,
I am the bird with the good son.

BABIES

Babies, babies,
before you can see more than light or darkness,
before your mothers have kissed your heads,
I come to you with news of dead and dying friends.
You so close to the miracle of life,
lend me a miracle to bring to my friend.
Babies, babies.
Once Death was a baby, he grasped God's little finger
to keep from falling— kicking and chortling
on his back, unbaptized, uncircumcised,
but invited to share sunlight and darkness
with the rest of us. Mother Death would nurse him,
comfort and wash him when he soiled himself
in the arms of the mourners and the heartbroken.

Older, Death took his place
at table beside his mother—her "angel."
They ate and drank from each other's mouth and fingers,
laughed at their private jokes. He could play for her
any musical instrument, knew all music by heart,
all birdsong, the purr, growl, snort, or whine
of each and every animal.
The story goes that, fat with eternal life,
all breath merely brushed and smoothed his wings,
older than his mother, he devoured her,
far from light or darkness.

Babies, at the moment of your first uncertain breath,
when your mother's magic blood is still upon you,
I come to you, the helpless ones still coughing
from miracles of birth.

Babies hardly heavier than clouds,
in desperation, for my friend, for a lark
I hold up the sac you broke through
as if it were *Saint Veronica's Veil*—
but no face is on it, no blood changed to wine,
no blood from marrow.
I hold up a heavy sack of useless words.
I shake a rattle to catch your eye or first smile.

PRAISE

for Yehuda Amichai

1.

Snow clouds shadow the bay, on the ice the odd fallen gull.
I try to keep my friend from dying by remembering
his childhood of praise to God, who needs us all. Würzburg:
the grownups are inside saying prayers for the dead,
the children are sent out to play—their laughter
more sacred than prayer. After dark his father
blesses and kisses him *Güttenacht*. He wakes
to go to school with children who stayed behind
and were murdered before promotion.

Now his wife lies beside him.
He may die with her head on his pillow.
He sings in his sleep:
"Her breasts are white sheep that appear on the mountain,
her belly is like a heap of wheat set about with lilies."
Awake, he says, as if telling me a secret:
"When metaphor and reality come together, death occurs."
His life is a light, fresh snow blowing across the bay.

2.

A year later in Jerusalem, he carries a fallen soldier
on his back, himself. The text for the day begins:
"He slew a lion in the pit in a time of snow."
Seconds, minutes, hours are flesh,
he tells me he is being cut to pieces—
if they had not made him turn in his rifle . . .
He sees I can not bear more of that.

18

Yet a little sleep, a little slumber, a little folding
of hands in sleep and we drink *to life*.
Chilled in desert heat, what keeps him alive:
soldiers—his wife, his son and daughter,
perhaps the ashes of a girl he loved in childhood.
Outside their window
a Sun Bird and Dead Sea Sparrow fly
from everlasting to everlasting.
Later he covers my head with his hands, blessing me,
later unable to walk alone he holds onto my hand
with so much strength he comforts me.

CHINESE PRAYER

God of Walls and Ditches, every man's friend,
although you may be banqueting in heaven
on the peaches of immortality
that ripen once every three thousand years,
protect a child I love in China
and on her visits to the United States,
if your powers reach this far, this locality.
You will know her because she is nine years old,
already a beauty and an artist. She needs more
than the natural protection of a tree on a hot day.
You have so many papers,
more than the God of Examinations,
more than the God of Salaries,
who is not for me, because I am self employed.
It may help you find her to know her mother
was once my bookkeeper,
her brother is a God in the family,
who at six still does not wipe his bottom.
Protect her from feeling worthless.
She is the most silent of children.
She has given me so many drawings and masks,
today I offered her fifty dollars for a painting.
Without a smile she answered,
"How much do you get for a metaphor?"
Sir, here is a little something to keep the incense burning,
remember her to the Almighty God whose character is Jade.

HERMAPHRODITES IN THE GARDEN

1.

After the lesson of the serpent there is the lesson
of the slug and the snail—hermaphrodites,
they prosper on or under leaves, green or dead,
perhaps within the flower. See how slowly
on a windless day the clouds move over the garden
while the slug and the snail, little by little, pursue
their kind. Each pair with four sexes
knows to whom it belongs, as a horse knows
where each of its four feet is on a narrow path:
two straight below the eyes, two a length behind.
There is cause and reason for,
but in the garden, mostly life befalls.
Each male female lies with a male female,
folds and unfolds, enters and withdraws.
On some seventh day after a seventh day they rest,
too plural for narratives, or dreams, or parables,
after their season. One by one they simply die—
in no special order each sex leaves the other
without comfort or desire.

2.

I open my hands of shadow and shell that covered my face—
they offered little protection from shame or the world.
I return to the garden, time's mash of flowers,
stigmas and anthers in sunlight and fragrant rain.
Human, singular, the slug of my tongue
moves from crevice to crevice, while my ear,

distant cousin of a snail, follows the breathing
and pink trillium of a woman who is beautiful
as the garden is beautiful, beyond joy and sorrow,
where every part of every flower is joy and sorrow.
I, lost in beauty, cannot tell which is which,
the body's fragrant symmetry from its rhymes.
I am surrounded by your moist providence.
A red and purple sunrise blinds me.

SHOES

Home, I bang the sand out of my shoes.
I haven't the craft to make a goat's-belly bagpipe
from a shoe or the art to play it,
but I can see my cold wet shoes
as unwept for bodies without a poet.
I speak for the leather ghosts of children.
I hold one up: a newborn infant without breath.
I cannot smack it into life. I face
mountains of shoes, endless lines of children
holding their parents' hands. I hold a shoe to my ear
like a seashell—hear a child's voice: "God is the old woman
who lived in a shoe, she had so many children
she didn't know what to do." I hear the cries of cattle
begging for mercy in the slaughter-houses,
I smell the stink of the tannery.
I am a shoemaker, not a bard.

BEAUTY IS NOT EASY

What are they but cattle, these butterflies,
their purple hides torn by barbed wire,
scarred blue, yellow and scarlet.
If they are not marked for slaughter
I cannot tell to whom they belong.
They are just stray cattle.
The sun does not witness,
the clouds do not testify.
Beauty does not need a public defender,
but I would listen to a serious defense
of beauty—tell me what happens to the carcass,
the choice cuts, everything useful:
hide, bones, intestines, fat.
Then talk to me of butterflies.

ANNUNCIATION

I saw a virgin who did not want to be
impregnated by words—but I do,
or did I see her pushing off the unwanted angel
when it was over, her humped-back cat hissing,
sensing perhaps the human, inhuman, natural son.
The loudest sound I ever heard came from within my ear:
babble and chaos, twins inside me, as if word and verb
from the beginning were without pause, stop, cesura—
all words meaningless, life without time and weather.
Did I hear my death conceived inside my ear,
like a child some call "the Savior"?

CREED

I salute a word, I stand up and give it my chair,
because this one Zulu word, *ubuntu*,
holds what English takes seven to say:
"the essential dignity of every human being."
I give my hand to *ubuntu*—
the simple, everyday South African word
for the English mouthful.
I do not know the black Jerusalems of Africa,
or how to dance its sacred dances.
I can not play Christ's two commandments on the drums:
"Love God" and "Love thy neighbor as thyself."
I do not believe the spirits of the dead
are closer to God than the living,
nor do I take to my heart
the Christ-like word *ubuntu*
that teaches reconciliation
of murderers, torturers, accomplices,
with victims still living.
It is not blood but *ubuntu*
that is the manure of freedom.

PROPHECY

An oracle told me
an elephant in a zoo
will pick up a child
in a red shirt, higher
than he has ever been
in a swing or a see-saw—
the trunk an S
over the elephant's head.
His father will drop
his ice cream cone,
the kid will wave to the world
hello, goodbye—
then swoosh across the moat.
That's the way it will happen.
You will call the mother
saying, "Darling,
I have something to tell you…"
the taste of chocolate
still in your mouth.
And you are the father
and you are the child.

THE LAST JUDGMENT

Pushing up through a hole in the red marble floor of heaven
a black prisoner sentenced to death,
shows his tattooed resurrected flesh:
a blue tear under the outside corners of his eyes,
on his arm two copulating dragons,
their eyes a woman's breasts,
a pierced bleeding heart on his back the size of an eagle,
his chest bears the face of Christ.
Anathema, it cannot be true such unlikely flesh rises to heaven.

Now in the maw of heaven
I see poor losers shrouded with eternal ink—
it's a little like whistling against Bach's B-minor mass,
there is so much ecclesiastical counterfeit money around:
the anti-Christ silver dollar, the St. Sebastian dime.
Asleep on the marble floor a drowned sailor,
at his knee a cock, his wrists ringed with barbed wire;
a woman walks in circles,
her body still scented with the lilies of death,
her mouth the shape of her lovemaking,
a wolf's head on her shoulder,
its nose nestled between her breasts.
Beneath a huge egg hanging from a cord,
a woman who seems to be mad
says she will die if she sleeps alone,
a vine of tiny roses runs down both sides of her belly
to her bush still moist, a large bee put where the hair begins —
on her back, lovers beneath a tree in full foliage
and the motto: *God is the name of my desire.*
Anathema, it cannot be true such unlikely flesh rises to heaven.

Is it true Jewish children with tattooed numbers on their arms
keep their religion even in heaven?
I look at my own flesh with the dyes of age,
the craquelure of love and capricios. How many nights
have I fallen asleep to the beat of the oars in a boat
with the adult passengers: summer, winter, autumn, spring—
not knowing who is the designer, who the boatman,
the needles writing all night like dreams,
awaking, as all of us, to an uncompleted world,
to the *Behold I am standing before Thy face.*

A REFRESHMENT

In our new society, all the old religious orders and titles are ice creams:
Rabbis, Priests, Mullahs, Gurus, Buddhists, Shiites, Sunni,
Dominicans, Franciscans, Capuchins, Carmelites—ice cream,
never before have the kids had such a choice of flavors,
never before have the Ten Commandments been so cool in summer.
I believe when the holy family rested on their flight to Egypt,
in the desert heat, they had a little mystical lemon or orange ice,
before chocolate and vanilla crossed the unnamed Atlantic.
Let us pray, not for forgiveness, but for our just dessert.

THE FILM CRITIC IMAGINAIRE

He found his good wife weeping alone
when their friend's infidelity was discovered.
She had long pretended her husband's playing around
was like filmmaking: a take here, a take there,
out of sequence, everything but their life together
would end up on the cutting room floor.
Now she wept at breakfast,
forgot to pick up his suit at the cleaners,
and wept over that.
Angered, he realized his friend's infidelity
had held a full-length mirror to his own,
that the friend's behavior was unacceptable:
he had inconvenienced the distinguished critic,
the reader, the anglophile, the man of the left.
For some days, my life was a fly buzzing around his head—
he swatted with the *Times*.

HOT NEWS, STALE NEWS

Thucydides tells us in an election year
Pisistratus, the Athenian tyrant,
wanting the protection of a god,
got the biggest beautiful woman he could find,
dressed her in silver and gold armor,
proclaimed her the goddess Athena
and drove through the streets of Athens
with the goddess at his side.
In our elections, every candidate
wants to be photographed
going to or coming from Jesus.
One declared "Jesus is in my heart,"
but when he refused to stay
the death warrants for a hundred or so,
his Jesus was silent.

Our presidential candidates,
like Roman emperors,
favor the death penalty,
but in two thousand years there is a difference.
No candidate would do it for fun, or think death
a competent sentence for cutting down trees
or killing deer, as in 18th century England.
It's not all blood and circus:
when Camus asked de Gaulle,
"What can a writer do for France?"
The President replied: "Write well!"
Have you heard what's new on the Rialto:
since Pope John Paul declared anti-Semitism a sin,
hell has been so crowded,
you can't find a decent room there at a hotel.
No one stoops to eloquence.

THE BLACK MAPLE

After an August Atlantic hurricane,
no curled brine-drenched leaf
was at first to Katherine's eye
a Monarch butterfly,
yet she telephoned the news:
flights of deceived Monarchs
had dropped down on her Black Maple
till she could not tell
leaf from butterfly.
In the morning when I arrived
only the tree of metaphor was there,
the butterflies gone to Mexico,
Katherine and her lover, soon to marry,
returned to Manhattan
to practice medicine and music.
Left behind by so much storm and flutter,
I have almost lost count of the seasons.

STOWAWAY

1.

Aging, I am a stowaway in the hold of my being.
Even memory is a finger to my lips.
Once I entered down the center aisle
at the Comédie Française, the Artemis of Ephesus
on my arm, all eyes on her rows of breasts and me.
"Who is this master of her ninety nipples?"
the public whispered.
Now the ocean is my audience,
I see in secret my last secret.

2.

Mid-December, my old felt hat that I could have imagined
myself leaving behind in a restaurant for eternity
blew out into the Atlantic. The damn thing so familiar
I saw myself wearing it even into the deep,
an aging Narcissus, in white foam and northern sunlight,
on my way to becoming a conch. It is like seeing music
this growing from flesh and bone into seashell:
undulating salts become a purple mantle,
and the almost translucent
bivalve of memory and forgetting closes.

HEART WORK

No moon is as precisely round as the surgeon's light
I see in the center of my heart.
Dangling in a lake of blood, a stainless steel hook,
unbaited, is fishing in my heart for clots.
Across the moon I see a familiar dragonfly,
a certain peace comes of that. Then the dragonfly
gives death or gives birth to a spider it becomes—
they are fishing in my heart with a bare hook,
without a worm—they didn't even fish like that
when the Iroquois owned Manhattan.
Shall I die looking into my heart, seeing so little,
will the table I lie on become a barge, floating
endlessly down river, or a garbage scow?

There is a storm over the lake.
There are night creatures about me:
a Chinese doctor's face I like and a raccoon I like,
I hear a woman reciting numbers growing larger and larger
which I take as bad news—I think I see a turtle,
then on the surface an asp or coral snake.
One bite from a coral snake in Mexico,
you'll take a machete and cut off your arm
if you want to live. I would do that if it would help.

I say, "It's a miracle." The Chinese doctor and the moon
look down on me, and say silently, "Who is this idiot?"
I tell myself, if I lie still enough I'll have a chance,
if I keep my eyes open they will not close forever.
I recall that Muhammad was born from a blood clot.
If I'm smiling, my smile must be like a scissors opening,
a knife is praying to a knife.

Little did I know, in a day, on a Walkman,
I would hear Mozart's second piano concerto,
that I would see a flock of Canada geese flying south
down the East River past the smokestacks of Long Island City.
I had forgotten the beauty in the world. I remember. I remember.

THE CELESTIAL FOX

1.

Death is a celestial fox that leaps out of his coffin,
tonight his tail sweeps away insects,
which the religious read as a sign:
the fox kills but does not end their lives.
Sometimes he stops, noses the air,
sings, showing his teeth.
I wish I just owed him money.

2.

When my two dogs and I run on the beach
innocently thinking we hunt the fox
because we see two eyes in the ocean
where the fox crouches at the foot of a great wave,
my dogs jump in barking at nothing I can see,
while the fox leaps into its true lair,
the moist den of every sexual act.
There he waits, waits with that I-told-you-so grin.

3.

I am a great cunt waiting for death to fuck me
between the golden thighs of endless morning,
swaddled in labia. American,
architect of my own destiny,
he shall not flatter me or marry me,
he shall not suck me or finger fuck me
though I am wet as the Mississippi,
death shall not slip it in.

POST-SURGERY SONG

My surgeon went harrowing like Christ in Hell,
dug a virtuous pagan tumor from my kidney.
"What do I look like inside?" I asked. "Just like every other,
except the distance from your kidney to your heart."
"Aah," I thought, "I have a certain lonely alley inside,
like the Vicolo della Bella Donna in Florence."
I thought I knew the catechism of the bladder,
the daily questions and answers, until blood clots
clogged my drain, once a Roman fountain.
My bladder swelled as if giving birth,
then for all the world—a razor blade in the anus.
I cried uncle. Christ and surgeon,
if you believe merely thinking it
is the same as driving in the nails,
leave my wound! Physician, heal Thyself.

SEPTEMBER 11: A FABLE

You caterpillars, who want to eat
until there is not one familiar leaf on our living tree,
in New York there are bees that will bore into your belly,
sleep with your striped velvet over their eyes,
with their feet on your heart,
that waking, will eat their way out of your soft belly.
I promise you would prefer
the quick sharp beak of a crow.
Become a butterfly.

THE WATCH

See, there are two snakes copulating.
Watch long enough, like Tiresias
you will become male and female,
no longer know your mother or father.
First in your mother's belly you had a snake's heart,
then chamber by chamber you grew a human heart.
Concealed at night, you do not see the body,
but the heat around the body—the subjunctive heat
after wish and desire. In the garden at night
you cannot tell snake from human.
The theater is dark, the play is a comedy:
someone before death is begging for ten last syllables.

FOR VIRGINIA ON HER 90TH BIRTHDAY

I know that at ninety sometimes it aches to sing
or to sit in a chair, that words, music, love and poetry
sometimes trip over each other.
Teach me to walk untrippingly past the grave,
to do the funny dance of the good long life.
It's easy as one, two, three. But what is one,
what is two, and where is three?
A good death is like a black butterfly
born too late during a mild winter.

THE STAFF

My office smells of Chinese women
from Beijing, Shanghai and Canada,
not flowers but flesh, the Forbidden City.
They speak Chinese so I will not understand
mostly about husbands or lovers.
I've taught them a little English poetry,
a little Western thought,
their lips alas have been soiled by my gutter words
for which they in turn have taught me the Chinese,
with characters and civilization.
Once they sang patriotic songs about terrible white devils
whose throats they cut and "O Canada."
The truth is they take good care of me
and I am grateful to *Wild Orchid*, *Harvesting*, and *Light*.
With rare Chinese seeds,
they have fertilized me.

LETTER TO AN UNKNOWN

Five centimeters, already Chinese,
in your mother's womb, pre-intellectual,
about sixty days. Sounds can see you,
music can see you. Fu Xu your father,
I introduce you to him, he is a painter
already saving for your education, preparing
to carry you on his shoulders to museums.
Zhu Ming your mother holds you close
as it is possible to hold a being close,
rare as an Empress, Freudian Chinese therapist,
she will teach you the joys and sorrows
of writing Chinese. May you spend
many happy years washing ink from your hands.
You have made the Great Wall of China bleed.
Who am I? Something like a tree
outside your window: after you are born,
shade in summer, in winter my branches
heavy with snow will almost touch the ground,
may shelter deer, bear, and you.

ALEXANDER'S FIRST BATTLE

Now that you are looking over the edge of the world,
who will blame you for refusing to exchange
your mother's warm breast for rubber and warm glass?
Will you ever again be content? There will be laughter
and music, the solace of small talk, the solace
of art or science, twelve-year-old whiskey.
You will search the earth through hard years
to find somewhere in a timeless bed, or Venice,
or God forbid in the backseat of a car,
the return of such contentment. Alexander,
fight the bottle, fight it with all your being.
I will fight at your side.

ALEXANDER FU

Surrounded by a great Chinese wall of love,
he is already three weeks old and has a name.
His mother combs his hair with her hand, nurses him.
Soon he will learn the tragic news: the world is not all love.
He has already begun to earn a living
a little of his poopoo was just put in a flower pot.
The least part of him bears the seal of his Manufacturer.

A RIFF FOR SIDNEY BECHET

That night in Florence,
forty-five years ago,
I heard him play
like "honey on a razor,"
he could get maple syrup
out of a white pine,
out of a sycamore,
out of an old copper beech.
I remember that summer
Michelangelo's marble
naked woman's breasts,
reclining Dawn's nipples—
exactly like the flesh I ached for.
How could Dawn behind her clouds hurt me?
The sunrise bitch was never mine.
He brought her down. In twelve bars of burnt sugar,
she was his if he wanted her.

DARK CLOUDS

From what breast does the milk of madness course?
We know the scene
where the inside became outside: lives of the saints,
battle scenes, Calvary, an exchange of the living
for the dead, the dead for the living. On a small scale
a homeless boy makes up his address, the death
of his mother still alive, his father's suicide.
He woos a woman, feigning he's going blind,
asked what he would farm – *rifles*, he smiles.
Some believe he never learned to pray out loud
so God would hear him. Speaking to himself
as if he were the Lord, he is two persons,
three, four, five, a multitude
climbing out of the mouth of a colossal shark.
His mother's breast wept, losing its milk.
He is the nursling of dark clouds. Truth was a storm.

2002, ALAS

Where are the birthday poems
for Stalin and Hitler,
the angelhair tarts for Franco?
Where are the sweets of yesteryear,
the party hats? Our revels are not over!
They are shooting rifles in the air
for bin Laden and Saddam.
Happy children
are making bombs of themselves
as never before.
Dreams of mass murder have only begun:
daydreams and wet dreams.
But where is the pastry?
Where are the poems?
Coming, coming, the children sing.
Coming, coming.

AN ARGUMENT

When you said that you wanted to be useful
as the days of the week, I said, "God bless you."
Then you said you would not trade our Mondays,
useful for two thousand years,
for the Seven Wonders of the ancient world.
I said, "Endless are the wonders
to which I can only say 'ah,' that our 'Ah'
who art in heaven can easily become the
'ah, ah' that comforts a baby." Then you said,
"Go make a living on metaphors for 'ah,'"
that I, a lunatic, secretly want to be
the Lighthouse of Alexandria,
a fifty-story-high collaboration
of art and science, a mirror of light
that might be seen five or ten days out to sea,
Poseidon standing on my shoulders,
the Library of Alexandria at my back,
all the wonders of Greek Africa.
I said, "Today is Monday. I want little more
than to be a hand-mirror my wife carries
in her purse with a hankie
to stop my hemorrhaging humility."

JUNE 21ST

Just when I think I am about to be tilted
on a table for death to eat—my friend arrives
playing a harmonica. It is my birthday.
He sings a little song that is a poem
written for the occasion.
How does he know the day I was born
the midwife laughed, enthusiastic
over the size of my head, chest and penis?
My mother must have told him.

My years are sheep, I shepherd them night and day,
I live with their "ba-ba."
They much prefer his harmonica to a pan-pipe.
Some years graze near me, others wander
across the valley out of sight.
I have two dogs, one dog can't do the job.
My 57th year keeps mounting my early years,
my 63rd year is giving it hard to my 57th,
my dogs are running in circles, barking for joy.

PSALM

God of paper and writing, God of first and last drafts,
God of dislikes, God of everyday occasions—
He is not my servant, does not work for tips.
Under the dome of the Roman Pantheon,
God in three persons carries a cross on his back
as an aging centaur, hands bound behind his back, carries Eros.
Chinese God of examinations: bloodwork, biopsy,
urine analysis, grant me the grade of fair in the study of dark holes,
fair in anus, self-knowledge, and the leaves of the vagina
like the pages of a book in the vision of Ezekiel.
May I also open my mouth and read the book by eating it,
swallow its meaning. My Shepherd, let me continue to just pass
in the army of the living, keep me from the ranks of the excellent dead.
It's true I worshiped Aphrodite
who has driven me off with her slipper
after my worst ways pleased her.
I make noise for the Lord.
My Shepherd, I want, I want, I want.

2

poems from

ASLEEP IN THE GARDEN

(1997)

&

THE INTELLIGENCE OF CLOUDS

(1989)

THE BATHERS

In the great bronze tub of summer,
with the lions' heads cast on each side,
couples come and bathe together: each touches only
his or her lover, as he or she falls back
into the warm eucalyptus-scented waters.
It is a hot summer evening and the last
sunlight clings to the lighter and darker blues
of grapes and to the white and rose plate
on the bare marble table. Now the lovers
plunge, surface, drift—an intruding elder
would not know if there were six or two,
or be aware of the entering and withdrawing.
There is a sudden stillness of water,
the bathers whisper in the classical manner,
intimate distant things. They are forgetful
that the darkness called night is always present,
sunlight is the guest. It is the moment
of departure. They dress, by mistake exchange
some of their clothing, and linger
in the glaring night traffic of the old city.

2.

I hosed down the tub after five hundred years
of lovemaking, and my few summers.
I did not know the touch of naked bodies
would give to bronze a fragile gold patina,
or that women in love jump in their lovers' tubs.

God of tubs, take pity on solitary bathers
who scrub their flesh with rough stone
and have nothing to show for bathing
but cleanliness and disillusion.
Some believe the Gods come as swans,
showers of gold, themselves, or not at all.
I think they come as bathers: lovers,
whales fountaining, hippopotami
squatting in the mud.

SONG OF ALPHABETS

When I see Arabic headlines
like the wings of snakebirds,
Persian or Chinese notices
for the arrivals and departures of buses—
information beautiful as flights of starlings,
I cannot tell vowel from consonant,
the signs of the vulnerability of the flesh
from signs for laws and government.

The Hebrew writing on the wall
is all consonants, the vowel
the ache and joy of life
is known by heart. There are words
written in my blood I cannot read.
I can believe a cloud gave us the laws,
parted the Red Sea, gave us the flood,
the rainbow. A cloud teaches kindness,
be prepared for the worst wind, be light of spirit.
Perhaps I have seen His cloud,
an ordinary mongrel cloud
that assumes nothing, demonstrates nothing,
that comforts as a dog sleeping in the room,
a presence offering not salvation
but a little peace.

My hand has touched the ancient Mayan God
whose face is words: a limestone beasthead
of flora, serpent and numbers,
the sockets of a skull I thought were vowels.
Hurrah for English, hidden miracles,
the A and E of waking and sleeping,

the O of mouth.
Thank you, Sir, alone with your name,
for the erect L in love and open-legged V,
beautiful the Tree of Words in the forest
beside the Tree of Souls, lucky the bird
that held Alpha or Omega in his beak.

HANNIBAL CROSSING THE ALPS

He urged his starving elephants upward into the snows,
the barges still smelling of Mediterranean brine,
packed with huddled troops, men of Carthage
in ice-covered armor, some wearing desert sandals
wrapped in leaves, elephants up to their necks in snow,
trumpeting, their trunks grabbing at crumbling clouds of snow.
The colossal gray boulders swayed, moved upward,
some tumbled back into the echoing ravines.
An avalanche, forests of ice fell on Africa.
In the morning soldiers gathered remnants of red and blue silk,
dry sardines and beans, gold goblets still sandy
from desert victories, live turtles meant for soup,
a tangle of chained goats and sheep meant for sacrifice.

O you runners, walkers, horsemen, riders of bicycles,
men of sense and small gesture, commuters like me,
remember Hannibal came down from the Alps
into the warm belly of Italy, and conquered.
It was twenty years later in another place,
after errors of administration and alliance,
that he poisoned himself. What is remembered?—
His colossal head asleep on the sand of Tunis,
a few dates, confusion between victories and defeats,
his elephants.

FOR MARGARET

My mother near her death
is white as a downy feather.
I used to think her death was as distant
as a tropical bird, a giant macaw, whatever that is—
a thing I have as little to do with
as the distant poor.
I find a single feather of her suffering,
I blow it gently as she blew
into my neck and ear.

A single downy feather is on the scales,
opposed by things of weight, not spirit.
I remember the smell of burning feathers.
I wish we could sit upon the grass
and talk about grandchildren
and great-grandchildren.
A worm directs us into the ground.
We look alike.

I sing a lullaby to her about her children
who are safe and their children.
I place a Venetian lace tablecloth
of the whitest linen on the grass.
The wind comes with its song
about things given that are taken away
and given again in another form.

Why are the poor cawing, hooting,
screaming in the woods?
I wish death were a whippoorwill,
the first bird I could name.

Why is everything so heavy?
I did not think
she was still helping me to carry
the weight of my life.
Now the world's poor are before me.
How can I lift them one by one in my arms?

RAINBOWS AND CIRCUMCISION*

1.

He might have made some other sign,
but it fitted his purpose to use sunlight
behind rain to make his sign of the covenant,
a rainbow, above the flood. What was in the sky
was suddenly moral, moonlight and passing clouds
were merely beautiful.

We answer the rainbow with an infant son,
cut a touch of ignorant flesh away.
The wordless infant stands on the Book
that separates him by the width of the pages
from the bookless ground.

Rainbow and mother, tell me who I am!
We might have used another sign,
a red dot on the forehead, or a scar on the cheek,
to show the world who we are,
but our sign is intimate, for ourselves
and those who see us naked—like poetry.

2.

Once in Rome, on a winter day after a rare snowfall,
I stood on a hill above the snow-covered arches,
columns and palm trees of the pillaged Forum.
Against a dark purple sky suddenly opened

*Rainbow and circumcision: each is a Biblical sign of the Covenant.

by shafts of sunlight, I saw two rainbows.
To see all that at the same time, and two rainbows,
was a pagan and religious thing: holy,
it was like the thunderous beauty of a psalm, and like
peeking through the keyhole with the masturbating slaves,
watching Hector mounted on Andromache. O rainbows!

LETTER TO THE BUTTERFLIES

1.

Dear Monarchs, fellow Americans,
friends have seen you and that's proof,
I've heard the news:
since summer you traveled 5000 miles
from our potato fields to the Yucatan.
Some butterflies can bear what the lizard would never endure.
Few of us can flutter away from the design:
I've seen butterflies weather a storm
in the shell of a snail, and come out of nowhere
twenty stories up in Manhattan.
I've seen them struggling on the ground.
I and others may die anonymously,
when all exceptionalism is over,
but not like snowflakes falling.
This week in Long Island
before the first snowfall, there is nothing left
but flies, bees, aphids, the usual.

2.

In Mexico
I saw the Monarchs of North America gather,
a valley of butterflies surrounded
by living mountains of butterflies—
the last day for many.
I saw a river of butterflies flooding
through the valley, on a bright day black clouds
of butterflies thundering overhead,

yet every one remained a fragile thing.
A winged colossus wearing billowing silk
over a sensual woman's body
waded across the valley,
wagons and armies rested at her feet.
A village lit fires,
and the valley was a single black butterfly.

3.

Butterflies,
what are you to me
that I should worry about your silks and powders,
your damnation or apotheosis,
insecticides and long-tongued lizards.
Some women I loved are no longer human.
I have a quarrel with myself for leaving my purpose,
for the likes of you, beauties I could name.

Sooner or later
I hope you alight on my gray stone
above my name and dates, questioning
my bewilderment.
Where is your Chinese God of walls and ditches?
Wrapped in black silk I did not spin,
do I hold a butterfly within?
What is this nothingness they have done to me?

DOG

Until the rain takes over my life I'll never change,
although I know by heart the Lord's Prayer
and the prayer Christ prayed to his father
in John, chapter 17, sanctifying himself.
Trying to convert me would be like teaching a dog to drive a car
just because it likes to go out for a drive—and save the poor mutt
from the greater or lesser vehicles of Buddhism.
On the other hand I am a dog that has been well treated
by his master. He kisses me and I lick his face. When he can
he lets me off the leash in the woods or at the beach.
I often sleep in his bed.

THE DECADENT POETS OF KYOTO

Their poetry is remembered for a detailed calligraphy
hard to decipher, less factual than fireflies in the night:
the picture-letters, the characters, the stuff
their words were made from were part of the meaning.
A word like "summer" included a branch of plum blossoms,
writing about "summer in a city street"
carried the weight of the blossoming branch,
while "a walk on a summer afternoon"
carried the same beautiful purple shade.

They dealt with such matters distractedly,
as though "as though" were enough, as though
the little Japanese woman with the broom
returning to her husband's grave to keep it tidy
was less loving than the handsome woman in the café
off the lobby of the Imperial Hotel
who kissed the inside of her lover's wrist.
In their flower arrangements, especially distinct
were the lord flower and emissary roses—

public representations now shadows.
Their generals and admirals took musicians
with them to war, certain their codes
would not be deciphered, in an age when hats
and rings were signs of authority and style.
They thought their secrets were impenetrable,
they thought they had the power to speak and write
and not be understood, they could hide the facts
behind a gold-leaf screen of weather reports.

It was Buddha who had an ear for facts:
coins dropping into the ancient cedar box,
hands clapping, the sound of temple bells and drums.
Codes were broken, ships sank, men screamed
under the giant waves, and a small hat
remained afloat longer than a battleship.

THE INHERITANCE

In Canada, on a dark afternoon,
from a cabin beside Lake Purgatory
I saw your two clenched fists in a tree—
your most recent rage—until I came to my senses,
and saw two small lighted glass lamps reflected
through a window onto the maple leaves.
Was it simply that I had stolen away
in the wilderness to go fishing on your birthday,
twelve years after your death, and you
less than your rusty pliers in my fishing box?

It is late August in the moral North.
To answer your first question,
I obey the fish and game laws
of New York State, Ontario and Quebec.
The odd branch has already turned red.
As for me I have turned inside out,
I cry for revolution against myself—
no longer red, I'm parlor pink and gray,
you, less than a thumb print on a page.

Matters still outstanding: you will not remember—
a boy, I cut school, sneaked out
to the 42nd Street library to read among readers
like a stray lion cub taken into a great pride.
I have kept your Greek grammar,
your 78 revolutions per minute
recording of Rossini's *Barber*
you played to stop me from crying,
almost my first memory.
Your "valuable papers," now valuable

only to me, I fed to a fire years ago.
Frankly I am tired of receiving letters from the dead
every day, and carrying you on my back,
out of the burning city,
in and out of the bathroom and bedroom,
you less than the smoke you wanted for a shroud.

Let us dance with Sarah behind the curtain
where God in his divine humor
tells Abraham Sarah will at ninety bear a son,
and she asks laughing within herself, "Will I have pleasure?"
Take one foot, then the other . . . Imitate a departure
if you make it not, and each going
will lend a kind of easiness to the next.
Father, you poisoned my father.
I am standing alone, telling the truth
as you commanded. (Without too many
of the unseemly details, like the sounds of you in bed
sucking, I thought, on fruit I later would not eat.)
You, less than a seed of a wild grape.

Today, in the last moments of light
I heard a fish, a "Musky," your nickname, break water.
As I sing my song of how you
will be remembered, if I could
out of *misericordia*, I'd tie you to the mast
and stuff your ears with wax. I regret
some parts of the body forgive, some don't. Father,
do not forget your 18 inch Board of Education ruler
on which I measured my penis, marking its progress.
You kept it on your desk before you till your old age.
One reason, perhaps, for the archaic Greek smile
I wore on my face through boyhood.
I never thought I'd dig your grave with laughter.

THE SWIMMER

I remember her first as a swimmer:
I saw my mother swimming, her arms reaching out
across giant ocean waves,
swimming through the breakers of the Atlantic.
I stood on the shore,
knowing almost nothing, unable to go to her—
dumbfounded by the wonder of it.
It was long before I could dress myself,
I was a little older than the weeping Chinese child
sitting alone in the rubble of the Nanking bombing—
barely old enough to be read to,
not able to tell time or count.
When I had that kind of knowledge, in her old age
she showed me herself naked, the tubes and the sack.
An hour later she said, "I must have been crazy."
Then she swam off again and never came back.
For a few days I awoke as that child again.
Now I have learned a kind of independence.
It is mostly in dreams she comes back, younger or older,
sometimes fresh from the joy of the swim.

THE LACE MAKERS

Their last pages are transparent:
they choose to see a world behind the words,
not the words, tatting, not stitching, an open page
of knots, never a closed fabric stitched by needles.
They see from the apples and pears on their plates
out to the orchard, from their tatting
to a bird with a piece of straw in his beak.
From combings transferred onto a running thread,
they make a row of rings resembling a reef,
a chain of knots, hammocks, fishnets,
things found in the hands of sailors.
Without looms, with their fingers,
they make bridal objects, knotted hairnets
seen in certain Roman bronze female portraits,
the twisted threads and knotted fringes of dusty
Egyptian wrappings, something for the cuff,
the lapel, the drawing room, nothing to wear in the cold.
They care about scrolls and variations,
a handkerchief, a design on a pillow,
a completed leaf, four ovals with connecting chains
becoming four peacocks, part of a second leaf,
as if they were promised the world would not
be destroyed, with or without paradise.

Noting the French for tatting is *frivolité,*
they make false chains, things obsolete, improper,
in search of new forms. They carry a thread
to a distant point, eight measured peacocks
of equal size with an additional thread
and the ends cut off. It has the heartless advantage
of being decorative in itself.

They sit and work in the aging light
like Achilles, hiding from his pursuers
in a dress, tatting among the women,
discovered by Odysseus who offered a trap of gifts:
the women picked hammered gold leaves and bracelets,
deserted by his Gods, Achilles chose a sword.
In any fabric there are constant beginnings
and endings with cut threads
to be finished off and cut out of sight.
The lacemakers read their yellow lace,
washing and ironing it is a fine art
—beautiful a straw basket filled with laundry
and language. But shall we call gossip prophecy?
Who will turn the hearts of the fathers to the children
and the hearts of the children to their fathers?
They are unworthy of undoing the laces of their own shoes.

LOST DAUGHTER

I have protected the flame of a match
I lit and then discarded
more than I cared for you.
I had little to go on:
a postcard that came for no reason,
forty years ago,
that told me of your birth and name,
but not who was your father.
I would never give
my child your name.
In the woods and ditches of my life you
are less than a wild flower.
If you have a garden I
am less than melted snow.
I never held your hand
and this is the only bed-time story
I will ever tell you.
No love, no prayer, no flame.

THE LESSON OF THE BIRDS

The Birds of Aristophanes taught me
before there was sky or earth or air,
before there was mystery or the unknown,
darkness simply entered from darkness and departed
into darkness: it moved back and forth as the sea does,
all shells, grottos and shorelines that were to be
were darkness.

Time weathered such things,
had a secret heavy underwing;
an urge toward a warm continuum,
its odor of nests made a kind of light.
Before there was pine, oak or mud, seasons revolved,
a whirlwind abducted darkness, gave birth,
gave light to an egg. Out of the egg of darkness
sprang love the entrancing, the brilliant.
Love hatched us commingling, raised us
as the firstlings of love. There was never
a race of Gods at all until love
had stirred the universe into being.

CLOUDS

Working-class clouds are living together
above the potato fields, tall white beauties
humping above the trees, burying their faces
in each other, clouds with darker thighs,
rolling across the Atlantic. West,
a foolish cumulus hides near the ocean
afraid of hurricanos.
Zeus came to the bed
of naked Io as a cloud,
passed over her and into her as a cloud,
all cloud but part of his face
and a heavy paw, half cloud, half cat
that held her down.
I take clouds to bed that hold me
like snow and rain, gentle ladies,
wet and ready, smelling of lilac hedges.
I swear to follow them like geese,
through factory smoke,
beyond the shipping lanes and jet routes.
They pretend nothing—opening, drifting, naked.
I pretend to be a mountain
because I think clouds like that.
A cloudy night
proclaims a condition of joy.
Perhaps I remember a certain cloud,
perhaps I bear a certain allegiance
to a certain cloud.

I HAVE COME TO JERUSALEM

I have come to Jerusalem
because I have a right to,
bringing my family who did not come with me,
who never thought I would bring them here.
I carry them as a sleeping child to bed.
Who of them would not forgive me?
I have come to Jerusalem to dream
I found my mother's mother by chance,
white-haired and beautiful, frightened behind a column,
in a large reception room filled with strangers
wearing overcoats. After forty-two years
I had to explain who I was. "I'm Stanley,
your grandson." We kissed and hugged and laughed,
she said we were a modern family,
one of the first to ride on trains.
I hadn't seen before how much she looked like
her great, great granddaughter. I remembered
that in her house I thumped her piano,
I saw my first painting, a garden, by her lost son.
I remembered the smells of her bedroom:
lace-covered pillows, a face-powdered Old Testament.
Then my dead mother and father came into the room.
I showed them whom I'd found and gave everybody chocolates,
we spoke of what was new
and they called me only by my secret name.

NEAR MACHPELAH/HEBRON

It was not a dream: a poet
led me down into the earth
where the sea in another age
had hollowed out a mountain.
He led me into a cave of marble cloud:
colossal backs, shoulders, thighs of reclining Gods.
Just above us a battlefield four thousand years old,
some olive trees and wild flowers.
I cannot believe these Gods need
more than an occasional lizard
or the sacrifice of a dove that comes to them
through jags and crevices.
Madness to think the Gods
are invisible, in us, and worth fighting for
—if they want anything, I suppose,
it is for the sea to come back again.

A GUEST IN JERUSALEM

On the grapes and oranges you gave me on a white plate: worry,
in the kitchen, day worry, in the bedroom, night worry
about a child getting killed; worry in the everyday gardens
of Jerusalem, on geraniums and roses from the time they bloom
in December, long as they live. In the desert wind
playing over the hair on a child's head and arms, worry.
In the morning you put on a soiled or clean shirt of worry,
drink its tea, eat its bread and honey. I wish you the luxury
of worrying about aging or money, instead of a child getting killed,
that no mother or father should know the sorrow
that comes when there is nothing to worry about anymore.

JERUSALEM: EASTER, PASSOVER

1.

The first days of April in the fields—
a congregation of nameless green,
those with delicate faces have come
and the thorn and thistle,
trees in purple bloom,
some lifting broken branches.
After a rain the true believers:
cacti surrounded by yellow flowers,
green harps and solitary scholars.
By late afternoon a nation of flowers: Taioun,
the bitter sexual smell of Israel,
with its Arabic name, the flowering red clusters
they call *Blood of the Maccabees*,
the lilies of Saint Catherine cool to touch,
beside a tree named *The Killing Father*,
with its thin red bark of testimony.
In the sand a face of rusted iron
has two missing eyes.

2.

There are not flowers enough to tell,
over heavy electronic gear
under the Arab-Israeli moon,
the words of those who see in the Dome of the Rock
a footprint of the Prophet's horse,
or hear the parallel reasoning
of King David's psalms and harp,
or touch the empty tomb.
It is beyond a wheat field to tell
Christ performed two miracles: first he rose,

and then he convinced many that he rose.
For the roadside cornflower
that is only what it is,
it is too much to answer
why the world is so, or so, or other.
It is beyond the reach
or craft of flowers to name
the plagues visited on Egypt,
or to bloom into saying why
at the Passover table Jews discard
a drop of wine for each plague, not to drink
the full glass of their enemy's suffering.
It is not enough to be carried off by the wind,
to feed the birds, and honey the bees.

3.

On this bright Easter morning
smelling of Arab bread,
what if God simply changed his mind
and called out into the city,
"Thou shalt not kill," and, like an angry father,
"I will not say it another time!"
They are praying too much in Jerusalem,
reading and praying beside street fires,
too much holy bread, leavened and unleavened,
the children kick a ball of fire,
play Islamic and Jewish
scissors cut paper, paper covers rock, rock breaks scissors.
I catch myself almost praying
for the first time in my life,
to a God I treat like a nettle
on my trouser cuff.
Let rock build houses,
writing cover paper, scissors cut suits.

4.

The wind and sunlight commingle
with the walls of Jerusalem,
are worked and reworked, are lifted up,
have spirit, are written,
while stones I pick up in the field
at random, have almost no spirit,
are not written.

Is happiness a red ribbon on a white horse,
or the black Arabian stallion
I saw tethered in the courtyard of the old city?
What a relief to see someone repair
an old frying pan with a hammer,
anvil and charcoal fire, a utensil worth keeping.
God, why not keep us? Make me useful.

WORK SONG

As full of Christianity
as the sea of salt,
the English tongue
my mother and father spoke,
so rich in Germanic tree and God worship
and old Romantic Catholic nouns,
does not quite work for me
at family burials or other,
as we say in English,
sacramental moments.

Although I know the Pater Noster
and Stabat Mater as popular songs,
I am surprised, when close friends
speak Hebrew, that I understand nothing.
Something in me expects to understand them
without the least effort,
as a bird knows song.
There is a language of prayers unsaid
I cannot speak.
A man can count himself lucky these days to be alive,
an instrument of ten strings,
or to be gently carried off by sleep and death.

What of belief? Like the tides
there is and is not a temple of words
on which work continues.
Unsynagogued, unschooled, but lettered,
I drag a block of uncut marble—
I have seen prayers pushed
into the crevices of the West Wall,

books stacked against the boulders,
ordinary men standing beside prophets and scoundrels.
I know the great stoneworkers can show the wind in marble,
ecstasy, blood, a button left undone.

EXCHANGE OF GIFTS

You gave me Jerusalem marble,
gypsum from the Judean desert,
granite from the Sinai,
a collection of biblical rock.
I gave you a side of smoked salmon,
a tape of the Magic Flute—
my lox was full of history and silence,
your stones tasted of firstness
and lastness, Jewish cooking.

You took me where a small boy came up to me
and asked me to dance him on my shoulders.
So we danced around Genesis and the Song
of Solomon. He clapped his hands to be riding
the biggest horse in Judea. I cantered lightly
around Deuteronomy, whirled around the Psalms,
Kings and Job. I leapt into the sweaty
life-loving, Book-loving air of happiness.

Breathless I kissed the child and put him down,
but another child climbed up my back.
I danced this one around Proverbs and that one
around Exodus and Ecclesiastes, till a child came up to me
who was a fat horse himself, and I had to halt.

What could I give you after that?
—When I left, a bottle of wine, half a bottle of oil,
some tomatoes and onions, my love.

SONG OF AN IMAGINARY ARAB

Until they killed my brother who killed you,
there were readers who read and smiled at:
From the rock of my heart a horse rose
that I should ride to follow them
the night they left by taxi
from the Damascus gate and fled toward Bombay.
My heart threw me off.
If only I had robes white enough,
but my robes were full of ashes and dust.
The rouge, lipstick and eyeshadows
you left on my flesh, I washed off before prayer.
My heart was gone, it looked back at me
from a distance, its reins bitten through.

Until they killed my brother who killed you,
there were readers who read and smiled at:
It is written, man was created not from the son but a blood clot.
When I am put in the grave and those who question the dead ask me,
"Was the blood drawn from the finger of God
or the heart or His tongue?"
I will not answer. I will say, "I have heard music so beautiful
it seemed the blood of the Lord."

Until they killed my brother who killed you,
there were readers who read and smiled at:
I know there is profit in God's word, in prayer rugs, in silk and wool,
blood of the lamb and spit of the worm.
A man who rose from barber to physician,
I prize most my grandmother's brass tray, pure as the sun
without etching or design, where I first saw the angel of mathematics,
the stateless angel of astronomy.

Until they killed my brother who killed you,
there were readers who read and smiled at:
Let an old Palestinian grandmother sit in the sun
beside an old Jewish grandmother; I'll bring them sage tea,
which in Hebrew is called something like "Miriam," because when Mary
was pregnant with Jesus sage tea comforted her.
The Jew said, "Respect is more important than the Talmud."

Until they killed my brother who killed you,
there were readers who read and smiled at:
I was admiring the girl on the balcony in Ramallah,
when the tear gas canister hit me in the head. I did not have time
to make the break between my thoughts and the attack on my head.
I thought it was a flower pot that fell off the balcony.
"Allahu akhbar!" I shouted. Someday the horse will fly.

Until they killed my brother who killed you,
there were readers who read and smiled at:
Love now is more dangerous than hate.

1998–2003

TO ARIEL, MY ARABIST FRIEND

Almost forty years after it happened
in the winter of 1947,
I saw a snapshot of my lost brother,
a Hellenistic Jew, sitting in a lifeboat,
wordless, a few yards from the shoreline of Palestine,
behind him a rusty sinking freighter,
his two years in a displaced persons' camp,
his two years in Treblinka.
With him in the boat, half a dozen Jews,
tired to death and hopeful, my brother
sat in the middle, somehow a little apart,
in a good overcoat, his gloved hands
in his pockets, thumbs out, his tilted fedora
brim up, a clean handkerchief in his breast pocket
as our mother taught him—still the *boulevardier,*
the *flâneur.* Knee deep in the water
to meet the boat and help them in, Mr. Kraus
from Frankfurt, to give the newcomers his card,
directing them to his Viennese pastry shop,
the best in Palestine.
And that other photograph of the entertainers of camp guards,
their horns and violins set aside,
getting a little rifle practice.
My brother washed more than one death
out of his handkerchief. For me as a child
his handkerchief was a white mouse
he set free in Europe's worst winter,
when it became inhuman to love.

Ariel, whose language am I speaking?

A VISIT TO KAUNAS

I put on my Mosaic horns, a pointed beard,
my goat-hoof feet—my nose, eyes, hair and ears
are just right, and walk the streets of the old ghetto.
In May under the giant lilac and blooming chestnut trees
I am the only dirty word in the Lithuanian language.
I taxi to the death camp and to the forest
where only the birds are gay, freight trains still screech,
scream and stop. I have origins here, not roots,
origins among the ashes of shoemakers
and scholars, below the roots of these Christmas trees,
and below the pits filled with charred splinters of bone
covered with fathoms of concrete. But I am the devil,
I know in the city someone wears the good gold watch
given to him by a mother to save her infant
thrown in a sewer. Someone still tells time by that watch,
I think it is the town clock.

Perhaps Lithuanian that has three words for soul
needs more words for murder—murder as bread:
"Please pass the murder and butter," gets you to:
"The wine you are drinking is my blood,
the murder you are eating is my body."
Who planted the lilac and chestnut trees?
Whose woods are these? I think I know.
I do my little devil dance,
my goat hooves click on the stone streets.
Das Lied von der Erde
ist Murder, Murder, Murder.

GHETTO THEATER, VILNIUS, 1941

Perhaps the players chose to wear something
about the person, a spoon, or since it was autumn
a large gold maple leaf that looked like a star of David
pinned to a shirt or blouse. The play was *One Can't Know Anything.*
Someone shouted: "You are play-acting in a cemetery!"
But they went on: "To sit, to stand, to lie on the ground,
is it better to close or open your eyes, to listen or not,
to speak or not to speak? Those are the questions."
Then a grave song: "I knew him well, Horatio.
Here hung the lips I have kissed I know not how often. . .
My Lord, I have some remembrances of yours."

Fifty-six years later in a sandlot where for three hundred years
the Great Synagogue stood, I watch children playing.
Perhaps God shows himself as hide and seek,
as wrestling, laughter, as children falling,
cutting their knees, and the rush of tears.

CENTAUR SONG

A creature half horse, half human,
my father herded his mares and women together
for song, smell and conversation. He taught me
to love wine, music and English poetry.
Like the Greeks he left the temple's interior
for priests, he observed outside
where he could see the pediment and caryatids.
If he saw a beauty out walking, or on a journey,
the proper centaur offered to carry her
over ice, or across a river—he'd bolt
to the edge of a wood, a place of sunlight,
the light itself stunned and entertained.
He slid her gently down his back,
held her to him with one hand and a hoof.
His hoofs cut: how could he touch with tenderness?
I feel his loneliness when I am just with horses,
or just with humans. There was a time
when he was tied to a tree,
so he could not go to either.
Now his city crushed deep in the ground
has disappeared in darkness
—which is a theme for music.
He licked the blood from a trembling foal,
he galloped back to his books.
The North Wind fathers,
which is why mares it is said
often turn their hindquarters to the wind
and breed foals without the aid of stallions.

HOMING

On a bright winter morning
flights of honking geese
seem a single being—
when my kind comes into such formation
I watch for firing squads.
I never saw a line of praying figures take flight.
On an Egyptian relief I've seen
heads of prisoners facing the same direction,
tied together by a single rope
twisted around each neck,
as if they were one prisoner.

I reach for a hand nearby.
An old dream makes me cautious:
An infant howling and pissing across the sky,
I was abducted by an eagle,
I remember the smell of carrion on its breath,
I was fed by and kissed the great beak.
Now a ridiculous, joyous bird rises
out of my breast, joins a flock of geese
in the sky's wilderness.
I'm left on earth with my kind.
They tie us throat-to-throat down here.
Honking, I pass over my own roof.

THE GEOGRAPHER

Before the geography of flowers and fruit,
he learned warmth, breast, wetness.
He came late to map-making, the arches and vaults
of the compass, a real and unimagined world
of prevailing winds, coastlines and mountains,
large bodies of water, rifts and faults,
altitudes and depth. Under the stars
he studied what he learned as a child:
that geography determined history,
that weather defined places, principal products.
He would simply walk out of doors to find
the Jews of the wind arguing with the Jews of the dust:
who shall be placed among the writings,
who among the prophets, what is legend
and what is visionary dream.

He studied the deserts, the once dry Mediterranean,
the colossal sculpture of Egypt and Assyria,
art that outweathered its gods.
Under *History* his notes linked the Armada—
the entry: "parched Castile had nothing,
had to conquer the world"—to Napoleon leading his armies
into the Russian winter—like a carload of sheep
each marked for slaughter with a splash of red paint.
They too seemed to have a leader.
He believed the molecular connection of all living stuff
since the beginning of life, made him less lonely—
no message, but a *cri de coeur.*

He had a small globe of the earth, he kept
inside another blue and silver globe of stars.

He learned and relearned touch, flesh and place,
the simple "where is," the colors of nearness,
the light and dark of naked bodies in repose.
He learned countries and cities as if
they were verbs, meaning beyond subject:
the word poetry came from the Greek "to make,"
the Chinese character for poetry is "to keep."
A fine day does not forget lightning and thunder. Facts:
it was not the fifty-degree-below-zero cold in winter,
or the ten-degree-below-zero cold in summer,
that caused one percent of the population to die each day
in the coal and blood-black snows of the Soviet arctic.
Memory makes any place part illusion.
Weather remembers, has a long memory of itself,
oceans, and landscape, nothing human.

He came to a certain calm in his studies:
the healing and destroying power of water,
the chaos of forest fires, followed by new unheard-of growth.
He noted bougainvillea and oleander
crossing continents like vacationing lovers—
he sketched the universe as an animal belly
full of exploding gases.
He had to make it all human as a bad joke.

He had cause to be frightened,
to turn his head to the beauty of it.
Under *The fruit trees of this world*, he wrote:
there's a murder for every apple, every peach, every pear,
beneath the oak a starving child for every acorn,
among the evergreens a lie for every pine needle.
These are the forbidden fruit.

CLOCKS

To Federico Zeri

1.

I pass a half-naked child
asleep on a marble slab in Grand Central Station.
I remember a painting: the *Infant Christ*
asleep on a red marble slab,
and another: the man, *Christ Dead,*
on the same red marble stone of unction.
The great iron clocks
in the railroad stations of Christendom
witness nothing,
they are simply above with their everydayness,
in natural, artificial and supernatural light.
I turn my head away from the faceless
puddles of drying urine
in the marble passageways
between nowhere and the street above.
I turn away from time's terrible sufficiency
that is, like God, in need of nothing whatsoever.
I do not know how to speak
for the poor of the world so hungry
God only appears to them as bread.
Without understanding I bite at passing minutes,
as animals in pain bite their wounds.

2.

Last June under the horologe of the Italian sky,
my mind full of timetables and illusions,
I went back to Siena after forty years,

faithful to something, the city scolded
by San Bernardino of the flaming heart
for loving the Madonna so much it had forgotten Jesus.
I saw a painting of the kneeling Archangel
announcing to Mary a child will be born to her:
she wears two delicate, looped earrings,
from which hang two little gold crosses,
signs of the Crucifixion that has not yet occurred.

Time is nothing—an echo;
night and day are only a foreshadowing.
I have not yet disappeared.

CLOWN

1.

He lived in flight from an apartment,
desolate as Beethoven's jaw. On the go
he could put his own life aside as an actor,
he drank till his feet turned purple
or into goat hooves. He could play the serpent,
Eve, Adam, the apple before or after it was bit.
He wandered beside himself, a figure far from himself
as orange rind: he could turn from David into Saul weeping—
to Absalom, his hair caught in a tree. He could play his own fool,
his own column of cloud, the presence of God.
He could throw himself out into the garbage,
or, like a child's top on a string
turn red and blue then whirl into a single color.
He played a Buddhist priest reading from his Book
into the ear of a corpse who hears
the reader's voice telling him all these visions
are his own unrealized, undiscovered forms,
the horrible furies and the calm
he must come to understand are his.

2.

"Far below the salt cliffs," he wrote in his Book of Hymns,
"the river's violin has emptied into the sea."
Only the man-bird flies from the Dead Sea to the Himalayas,
from the ancient dead shrouded in poetry
to the never-ending ice so thick, the dead
are ritually butchered and fed to vultures that
surrounded by haloes of the sun, rise like doves
out of the jeweled snow. In the glacial silence
a man's leg-bone makes a sweeter whistle than your ram's horn.

3.

To bathe at birth, marriage and death, "a rule in Tibet,"
was not enough even for him. "No one has ever slid down
the Himalayas so fast," he said in a coarse aside.
Unteachable, he learned, he fell
more like Richard II than Adam,
like glistening Phaeton wanting the manage of unruly horses.
In a farce he came closest to the stinking breath
of his own mortality, trying to lift a snapping turtle off a busy road,
it bit into his shoe, he fell back out of the blue sky—
broke his ankle and elbow.

4.

What did he know that no one knew?
The care he wanted to give, that no one else would give.
He had lived to sing to his dying mother
from beside her bed. Now memory is his mother,
she keeps his life from burning off like a morning mist.
One blue tear at the corner of his right eye
a red tear at the left,
he tried to fly with a chicken wing. He pretended
to play Mozart on a violin without lessons.
He bought himself a fiddle and a bow
strung with circus-horse hair, an earthly bow, not a rainbow.
Who was he to know so many tunes?
He just played his everyday music—
he would never wrap the letters of the holy name
around his fingers. He wrote a song that began:
"I fall back from making love
to the kind of day it is. . . ."

SONG OF INTRODUCTION

Ancient of Days,
I hear the sound and silence, the *lumière*
of molds, disease and insects, I believe poetry
like kindness changes the world, a little.
It reaches the ear of lion and lamb, it enters
the nest of birds, the course of fish, it is water
in the cupped hands of Arab and Jew.
Reader, in writing this I become you, I must awake
in your darkness and mine and sleep with your sleep
and mine. If ever in writing I become a tree
I am not likely to set myself afire,
as a stone I will not stone the innocent
or guilty, my Arabs and Jews will do
what my imagination wishes: make peace.
If you bring the flood, I will dam you up
as a river, though I do it on lined paper,
with an awkward hand. I believe something is thundering
in the mold, churning the hives of insects,
that the breath of every living creature mixes
in a kiss of life, that the killer's breath may taste of honey,
that when the forms of music change,
the state may tremble.

THE BATTLE

When Yahweh spoke to me, when I saw His name
spelled out in blood, the pounding in my heart
separated blood from ink and ink from blood,
and Yahweh said to me, "Know your soul's name
is blood and ink is the name of your spirit.
Your father and mother longed with all their hearts
to hear my Name and title given to every generation."
When I heard the clear difference between my spirit
and my soul, I was filled with great joy,
then I knew my soul took the hillside
under its own colors, in the mirror red as blood,
and that my spirit stood its ground in the mirror
that is black as ink, and that there raged
a ferocious war in my heart between blood and ink.
The blood was of the air and the ink of the earth
and the ink defeated the blood, and the Sabbath
overcame all the days of the week.

(after Abraham Abulafia, 13ᵗʰ-century Hebrew poet)

100

YOU AND I

You are Jehovah, and I am a wanderer.
Who should have mercy on a wanderer
if not Jehovah? You create and I decay.
Who should have mercy on the decayed
if not the creator? You are the Judge
and I the guilty. Who should have mercy
on the guilty if not the Judge? You are All
and I am a particle. Who should have mercy
on a particle if not the All?
You are the Living One and I am dead.
Who should have mercy on the dead if not
the Living One? You are the Painter and Potter
and I am clay. Who should have mercy on clay
if not the Painter and Potter? You are the Fire
and I am straw. Who should have mercy on straw
if not the Fire? You are the Listener
and I am the reader. Who should have mercy
on the reader if not the Listener? You
are the Beginning and I am what follows.
Who should have mercy on what follows
if not the Beginning? You are the End and I am
what follows. Who should have mercy
on what follows if not the End?

(after an anonymous 13ᵗʰ-century Hebrew poem)

THE ALTAR

One by one I lit the candles of nothingness,
a candle for each nostril, the eyes, and ears,
a candle for the mouth, penis and anus.
Under the clouds of nothingness,
below the flaming particles of the universe,
I stood beside the nothing tree,
I ate my fill.

To God I swore nothing.
In the blood and fires of without
nothing was written. I heard the sermons of nothing
and I knew nothing had come, and would come again,
and nothing was betrayed.

I called prayer
the practice of attention: nothing was
the balance of things contrary.
Disobedient, I did not make
the sacrifice of the lamb or the child.

My candelabrum was ablaze.

IN FRONT OF A POSTER OF GARIBALDI

1.

When my Italian son
admired a poster of Garibaldi
in the piazzetta of Venice,
a national father in a red shirt,
gold chain, Moroccan fez and fancy beard,
I wished the boy knew the Lincoln
who read after a day's work,
the commoner, his honesty.
My knees hurt from my life and playing soccer—
not that I see Lincoln splashing with his kids
in the Potomac. Lord knows where his dead son led him.

2.

My son tells me Fortuna could have put
Lincoln and Garibaldi in Venice—
Garibaldi in red silk, Lincoln,
in a stovepipe hat black as a gondola.
My son mimics Garibaldi:
"Lincoln you may be the only man in the piazza
to log down the Mississippi
and walk back the 1500 miles to Illinois
but you are still a man who calls all pasta macaroni.
How do you know where you are going?
Your shoes are straights, no lasts,
no right or left, no fashion, white socks.
How can the President of the United States
make such a *brutta figura?*"

3.

I can't speak for Lincoln,
any more than I can sing for Caruso
—toward the end when Caruso sang,
his mouth filled with blood.
Not every poet bites into his own jugular:
some hunger, some observe the intelligence of clouds.
I was surprised to see a heart come out
of the torn throat of a snake. I know a poet
whose father blew his brains out
before his son was born, who still leads his son
into the unknown, the unknowable.

4.

My son tells me I must not forget
Garibaldi fought for liberty in six countries
including Uruguay, he refused the command
of a corps that Lincoln offered, asked
to be head of the Union armies and for
an immediate declaration against slavery,
he was the "King's flag," defeated
the papal armies in 1866,
which gave the Jews equality in Italy.

5.

I've always had a preference
for politics you could sing
on the stage of the Scala.
I give my son Lincoln and Garibaldi
as guardian angels.
May he join a party and a temple
that offer a chair to the starving and unrespectable.

104

We come from stock that on the day of atonement
asks forgiveness for theft, murder, lies, betrayal,
for all the sins and crimes of the congregation.
May he take his girls and bride to Venice,
may the blessings come like pigeons.
Lincoln waves from his gondola and whispers,
"I don't know what the soul is,
but whatever it is, I know it can humble itself."

LENIN, GORKY AND I

1.

That winter when Lenin, Gorky and I
took the ferry from Naples to Capri,
nobody looked twice
at the three men having a lemon ice
in Russian wool suits hard as boards.
Behind us, a forgetful green sea,
and the Russian snows storming the winter palace.
We descended, three men a bit odd,
insisting on carrying our own suitcases
heavy with books: Marx, Hegel, Spinoza.
We took the funicular
up the cliffs of oleander and mimosa,
yet through the fumes of our cheap cigars
we observed how many travelers had come
to Capri with a beauty. Lenin to Gorky:
"In Moscow they'd kill on the streets for the girl
who showed me my room."
Within an hour of our arrival
we were sitting in the piazza drinking fizz,
longing for the girls strolling by:
a mother, a sister, a daughter.
You could smell an ageless lilac in their hair.
Lenin warned, raising our level from low to high,
"Love should be like drinking a glass of water . . .
You can tell how good a Bolshevik she is
by how clean she keeps her underwear."

2.

It was then I split with the Communist Party.
Gorky welcomed the arrival of an old flame
from Cracow. Lenin bought white linen trousers
but would not risk the Russian Revolution
for what he called "a little Italian marmalade."
It was I who became the ridiculous figure,
hung up in the piazza like a pot of geraniums,
not able to do without the touch, taste and smell
of women from those islands in the harbor of Naples.

FOR JAMES WRIGHT

Hell's asleep now.
On the sign above your bed
nothing by mouth, I read *abandon hope.*

You sleep with your fist clenched,
your tongue and throat swollen by cancer
make the sound of a deaf child
trying to speak, the smell
from the tube in your belly
is medicinal peppermint.

You wake speechless.
On a yellow pad your last writing
has double letters—two Zs and Ys in "crazy,"
you put your hand on your heart
and throw it out to me.
A few pages earlier you wrote
"I don't feel defeated."

In your room without weather,
your wife brings you more days,
sunlight and darkness, another summer,
another winter, then spring rain.

When Verdi came to his hotel in Milan
the city put straw on the street
below his window
so the sound of the carriages
wouldn't disturb him—if I could,
I'd bring you the love of America.

I kiss your hand and head, then I walk out on you,
past the fields of the sick and dying,
like a tourist in Monet's garden.

SONG FOR STANLEY KUNITZ

Creature to creature,
two years before we met
I remember I passed his table
at the Cedar Tavern.
He who never knew his father
seemed to view all strangers
as his father's good ghost,
any passing horse as capable
of being Pegasus, or pissing
in the street.
I who knew my father
was wary of any tame raccoon
with claws and real teeth.

At our first meeting forty years ago,
before the age of discovery,
I argued through the night
against the tragic sense of life;
I must have thought God wrote in spit.

I keep a petrified clam, his gift, on my desk.
These gray rings and layers of stone,
shape of a whale's eye, are old as any desert.
Measured against it, the morning, the Hudson River
outside my window are modern and brash,
the star of David, the cross, the hand of Fatima,
are man-made weather vanes.
My clamstone has weight and lightness.
It is my sweet reminder that flesh,
perhaps love, can remain in the natural world
long as poetry, tides, phases of the moon.

Tomorrow I shall wear it in my right eye,
a monocle for my talk on the relationship
between paleontology and anthropology.

Bless Celia, the cat of his middle years,
with her ribbons and hats, her pagan smile.
Bless the bobcat that was his in boyhood,
that killed a police dog in battle
on Main Street, Worcester, lost a foot for it
and had to be shot. A child with a leaf in his head,
he walked through Scabious Devilsbit,
Marshrag wort, Vernal grass
until the meadows wept. Bless his first garden,
his bird feeder still there after 81 years.
Did any of his long-forgotten kindnesses
alter history a little?

What a *Luftmensch* he might have been,
his feet barely touching Commercial Street,
dancing home at three in the morning
with an ocean of money!
But how could he face the moon or the land
beside his house without a garden? Unthinkable.
I think what is written
in roses, iris and trumpet vine
is read by the Lord God.
Such a place of wild and ordered beauty
is like a heart that takes on the sorrows
of the world . . . He translates into all tongues.

LOWELL

He needed to be held, so his country
held him in jail awhile, non-violent,
manic New Englander. In conversation
his hands moved across sentences, a music
of almost indiscernible Latin consonants
and Tennessee cake-walking vowels.
What was sight but a God to fool the eye?
Although he looked at you he stared away,
his eyes moved across some distant lawn
like the eyes on a peacock's tail.
Now his life of love, books and nightmares
seems 19th century American allegory,
without the lofty language.
Could he imagine the lives of those who read
without the slightest attention to form,
the lives of readers of newspapers, books
of passing interest, or nothing at all—
their deaths a slip of the tongue?
A generation that might kill itself
gathered in him as if he were a public place:
to pray, agitate and riot. The man and flame he was
waved back and forth in the wind,
became all tongue. Falling off his ladder
in Ireland his last morning, "Whack. Huroo.
Take your partners," caught without time
to tell what happened, locked in a museum,
he tried to break through the glass door.
That evening in Manhattan he fell silent
on the floor of a taxi, the meter running.
Gluck said of early opera, "It stinks of music."
Cal, your life stank of poetry . . . "Buzz, buzz, he said,
a few bring real honey to the hive."

NEW YORK SONGS

1.

When I was a child, before I knew the word for love,
before I remember a tree or a field,
I saw an endless gray slate afternoon coming,
I thought a bird singing in the sun
was the same as a dog barking in the dark.
A pigeon in a blizzard fluttered
against the kitchen window,
my first clear memory of terror—
I kept secret.

Last winter I hung a gray and white felt seagull
from the cord of my window shade, a reminder
of good times near Montauk, Chekhov and impossible love.
Today, I saw through the window
a living seagull glide toward me
then in an instant disappear—what a rush of life.
I remember its hereness,
while inside the room
the senseless symbol,
little more than a bedroom slipper,
dangled on a string.

2.

Later, on the way to visit a physician,
a friend, who would soon suddenly die,
I saw a pigeon on a heap of rubble
standing more like a gull,
others in wild flight

searching the wreckage
of two Times Square theaters,
razed to build a hotel.
They were looking for their roof,
their nest, their young,
in the hollows of broken concrete,
in the pink and white dust,
they fluttered around the wrecking ball
that still worked the facade,
the cornice of cement Venetian masks.

I'll be no messenger for pigeons.
It means little that I see
the resemblance
between their markings
and the yellow, red and blue dots
that speckle the trout and butterfly.
They must be born of a universal egg,
as Clytemnestra and blue-eyed Helen
were born of a mortal mother and a swan.
The roof, a giant bird of tarpaper,
takes its last breaths on the broken stage.
There are no tragic pigeons.
I mourn my sweet friend
fallen among the young,
unable to sustain flight,
part of the terrible flock,
the endless migration
of the unjustly dead.

ELEGY FOR MYSELF

The ashes and dust are laughing, swaddled,
perfumed and powdered, laughing at the flowers,
the mirrors they brought to check his breath,
and he no longer singular.
Who will carry his dust home in merriment?
These things need a pillow, a wife,
a dog, a friend. Plural now he is all the mourners
of his father's house, and all the nights and mornings too.
Place him with "they love" and "they wrote,"
not "he loves" and "he writes." It took so much pain
for those S's to fly off. It took so much trouble
to need a new part of speech. Now he is
something like a good small company of actors;
the text, not scripture, begins, "Who's there?"

THE POOR OF VENICE

The poor of Venice know the gold mosaic
of hunger, the grand architecture of lice,
that poverty is a heavier brocade
than any doge would shoulder. To the winter galas
the poor still wear the red silk gloves of frostbite,
the flowing cape of chilblain.

The winged lion has his piazza, lame dogs
and pigeons with broken wings have theirs.
Let the pigeons perform for dry corn
their Commedia dell'Arte in the palms of tourists.
The rich and poor don't share a plate of beans.

There used to be songs about squid and sardines
in love the poor could make some money from.
A boy in bed with his family asks for a violin,
his father leaps up,
"Violin, violin, I'll buy you a shovel!"
Moored in the dark canals of Venice,
gondolas for prisoners, for the sick,
gondolas for the dying, the hungry,
tied to poles by inescapable knots
looped by Titian.

Salute an old Venetian after his work.
Eating his polenta without quail, he sits
on a slab in the freezing mist, looking back
at the lagoon and his marble city:
years of illusion, backache, sewerage and clouds.

SONG OF IMPERFECTION

Whom can I tell? Who cares?
I see the shell of a snail protected by a flaw
in its design: white is time, blue-green is rot,
something emerging in the rough dust, the unused
part of a shape that is furious and calm.
In aging grasses, knotted with their being,
the snail draws near the east bank of the pond,
not because that is where the morning sun is,
but out of coastal preference, raising
a tawny knotted counterwhirl
like a lion cub against its mother's haunch,
anus of a star. But let the conch stand
in the warm mud with its horn become an eye,
suffering the passion of any snail:
a miraculous birth, a death, an empty tomb.
I'd follow such a horned eye, its spores, webs,
wet ferns and corals, lip-foot after lip-foot, beyond
the dry wall of my life, backward
into the sacramental mud, where the soul begins to reason—
as on that afternoon Aristotle dissecting
squid proclaimed "the eternity of the world."

THE POET

He stared at a word and saw his face,
in every noun and every verb—his own face.
He could understand if he saw his face
in words like *ocean*, or on a blank page
or in anything that might mirror him,
but he saw his own face in *buts* and *ands*,
in *neither nor*, in *which* and *whose* and *what*.
In the names of others living and dead
he saw his own face.
The moment his senses came into play,
at the very edge of any perception, in light or darkness,
the word became his flesh
with his obscene mouth, his poisonous eyes.
Secretly he drew close to certain words
he hoped might not be his face, words he misspelled
in languages he barely knew, but every letter
was hair and tooth. What was not his face
was wordlessness—wordless tears, wordless laughter—
that never came to vowel or consonant.

ALLEGORY OF EVIL IN ITALY

The Visconti put you on their flag: a snake
devouring a child, or are you throwing up a man
feet first? Some snakes hunt frogs, some freedom of will.
There's good in you: a man can count years on your skin.
Generously, you mother and father a stolen boy,
to the chosen you offer your cake of figs.
A goiter on my neck, you lick my ear with lies,
yet I must listen, smile and kiss your cheek
or you may swallow the child completely. In Milan
there is a triptych, the throned Virgin in glory,
placed on the marble below, a dead naked man
and a giant dead frog of human scale on its back.
There's hope! My eyes look into the top of my head
at the wreath of snakes that sometimes crowns me.

THE STARTLING

When I saw the Greek hunter
painted on the fifth-century red-figured pot
was changed into a startled fawn
because he watched a goddess bathe naked,
and that his own dogs tore him to pieces,
I had already changed from myself
to another self, further apart
than man from fawn.
When coming out of my self, I woke you
in the middle of the night to carry you off
to the sea, I stopped three times
to ravish you; you took me beyond my life,
raced me from great distance to great distance,
till helpless I fell in your lap
and said I was near death.
You lifted the heavy beast's head,
still snorting and groaning, kissed me
and washed your blood from my face,
stroked me and called me "sweet one"—
then you sang your siren song,
told me how I would be remembered,
that sleep and death were brothers,
that the sirens defeated by poetry
were changed into the great boulders
on which the city of Naples,
so well known to lovers, was founded.
I kissed you and you asked gently,
since you were young and I was not,
what Dido asked Aeneas
who was soon to go to war:
"Will you leave me without a son
of your name?"

120

ALLEGORY OF SMELL

His smile says he has had the smell of it,
flying the bitter end of a rooster tail
above his hat. In a torn army jacket
an old soldier pounds the tavern table.
They bring him an onion, garlic and a rose.
He discards the rose. He says, "To hell and back
a man stinks of what he is." He shouts:
"I myself am a sack of piss—thanks to brandy
mine smells like an apple orchard."
He remembers the gardens of women:
summer women, when they pass, enter
a man's soul through the nostrils, the consolation
the good Lord provides old soldiers.
A smell can be as naked as a breast.
His red eyes shine with tears from the onion he eats.

LULLABY

I hear a Te Deum of. . . "Who are you to think. . .
touch religion like a hot stove,
hide bad news and the dead. . . a fool will light candles,
a fool will bless the children, a fool is ceremonious."

I see my first roadside wildflowers,
the lake—every sunfish nibble is a kiss.
On a summer afternoon
the clouds and I are useless brothers;
Eros carves his bow with a kitchen knife.

I read by the light of fire blazing in their hands:
my father who I thought would die forever,
my mother who I thought would live forever.
I won't forget the child who could not speak his name,
Rossini arias, the condoms on the floor,
the studying, the sweet and sour of moral purpose,
under a frowning etching of Beethoven.
The cuckoo clock was moved from room to room.
Age ten, I flew a red flag for revolution
in my bedroom and yearned for a better world.

I've made my family into an entertainment.
Once I named their symbols: the sewing basket,
fruits and animals, as their attributes.
I could show us as we were at home,
walking across a New York street or at the ocean
each brooding alone in the sand.
There is a lullaby children sing to the old.
The truth is, now in death we hold hands.

KRILL*

The red fisherman
stands in the waters of the Sound,
then whirls toward an outer reef.
The krill and kelp spread out,
it is the sea anemone that displays the of,
the into, the within.
He throws the net about himself
as the sea breaks over him.
The krill in the net and out of it
follow him. He is almost awash
in silver and gold.
How much time has passed.
He believes the undulation of krill
leads to a world of less grief,
that the dorsal of your smelt,
your sardine, your whitebait, humped
against the ocean's spine, cheers it
in its purpose.
The krill break loose, plunge down
like a great city of lights. He is left
with the sea that he hears
with its *if* and *then*, *if* and *then*, *if* and *then*.

*a small crustacean, basic food of the whale

THE PUBLIC GARDENS OF MUNICH

The park benches, of course, are ex-Nazis.
They supported the ass of the SS
without questioning; the old stamp *Juden Verboten*
has been painted out.
The only signs of World War II, photographs,
displayed at the classical Greek museum,
show its roof bombed, now handsomely repaired,
although the sculpture itself has been overcleaned
by a very rough hand.

But the flowers are the children of other flowers,
the hypocrite roses and the lying begonias,
part of gardens so sentimental, so ordered,
they have nothing to say about freedom and beauty,
nothing to say about the burning bush.
They should see the flowers on the hills of Judea,
pushing between limestone and gypsum, ordinary
beautiful flowers with useful Hebrew names,
useful to children, old people, everyone,
their colors and grace, the poetry of them,
page after page.

A man can hide under his shirt
flowers made by metal and fire, stems cut,
neck wounds, missing bone, history
of generations, new branches grafted
onto old stumps.
The saying goes in the streets of Munich:
"Wear a good overcoat." Everyone knows,
you can put a dead body under a handkerchief.
Every handkerchief's a grave,

that's why so many gentlemen wear clean handkerchiefs
in their breast pockets. For the ladies, lace gloves
serve the same purpose—blue handkerchiefs, pink gloves,
green, lavender *und so weiter* are symbolic—
but you have to really know—white for Jew,
blue for Jew, green for Polack, pink for—
you'd better watch out, a little joke.

This year in the Spanish garden during Carnival
someone decapitated a donkey,
Renaissance symbol of the Old Testament,
or perhaps the meaning is, as the TV
commentary said: the donkey
stands for a fifteenth-century Jew,
or was it just *Kinderspiele*,
a game like this hee-haw.

MON PÈRE*

1.

After his death, her blood was glass
that shattered within her, my mother could not bleed
or heal. Once in the moonlit snows of France
she offered his dark soul her breast.
Now for her night meal, she stares
at a little fish and vegetables
ladled out of being,
as if they were a family crucifix.
Her work: etchings she holds up
(the whorls of her fingertips stained by acid)—
small, detailed views of mountains,
coastlines, complex clouds.
Sometimes you simply have to repeat
a little of the design of the creator—
nothing whatsoever made by man.

2.

My father could turn the word being
into begging, into bed, into please,
his son twists his legs around his own neck,
man of rope, no farther from my father
than where a tree may root;
I hang by my teeth
from a rope fixed to the roof,
while the 19th century French band below
plays *Art Is the True Religion*.
I bite a stranger's leather tongue.

The poet Paul Celan threw himself into the Seine in 1970; his son is an aerialist and a juggler.

126

3.

Juggler as poet, not the fire-eater,
not the fat man, like father, like son:
my chilly eyes and two hands keep three, four, ten,
twenty clubs or white plates going in air,
like after likes, the sins of the fathers,
red silk balls, kept up in the air.
I throw up household effects: his Hebrew Bible,
a yellowing toothbrush, shoes and ties,
his murdered family, his thanks
that it happened to them, not to him.
I fling up against the crowd
my father's head, red silk balls, white plates
of the unthinkable, a way of mourning,
Jerusalem remembered, synagogue as circus.
Prophecy has fallen to sleight of hand,
better to learn magic, better to change
two blue eggs in a lacquer box
into three fluttering white doves.

4.

Hanging on by a hair,
on that night different
from all other nights,
he could not pull himself out
by a breath.
He was something like hair
with feeling only at its roots.

Coming from a musical family,
he could not bear to hear music,
he could not stop

his constant, endless bleeding
in private, in public,
on the bread he ate,
on my mother's face.
Drowning simply wet him
and sent his life and blood off
in water like smoke.
His fingers were dactyls again.

A fisherman found him
decomposing
far below Notre Dame Cathedral.
They quickly washed their hands of him.
In the chapel of virtues
the Virgin wept for her son
surrounded by images
of women without lives:
Temperance, Fortitude, Justice
and Prudence with her three eyes
to see past, present and future.

Once he knew the work of One
perfect in knowledge,
the balancer of clouds
—his garments were warmed
when Jehovah quieted the earth
with the South wind.
The language of the psalms
has a different word
for why asked in the past
and why asked in the future.
Why lose the rest of spring, mon père?

SOME FLOWERS

For Irving Howe

In a world where you are asleep with your fathers,
in that part of the forest where trees read,
your tree still reads to us. Tonight your branches bend over
Conrad, Trotsky, Saba,
the evergreen Irish.

Joyce hated flowers,
his wife put a house plant on his grave.
There are no socialist flowers
yet the balmiest wind favors
a more even distribution of wealth.
Some have seen among the flowers religious orders,
proved a rose a Christian,
while of course they pruned away the Jew.

It is easier for me to believe flowers
know something about wages and hours,
a fair day's pay for a fair day's work in the sun,
than to believe in the resurrection of the flesh.

When you died, the Amalgamated Clothing Workers
of America published a notice
of their mourning and sent flowers.
Your last sweet note that reached me after your death,
I left on the dashboard in a book,
the way they used to press dry flowers.
As I drove along in Canada,
it flew out of the window—
I thought it was a bill.

LINES FOR A STAMMERING TURKISH POET

To Edouard Roditi

1.

When he was a child, he thought of sea birds as Moslem,
fidgety land birds as Christians and Jews;
in his village, when a man approached, the women
squatted down in the roadside and turned away,
the branches of pomegranate and orange trees
heavy with fruit, lowered to the ground. . . .
In the sky-blue copybook of his school days
he was compelled by revolution to change
from an Arabic alphabet, with its gardens and forests,
to twenty-nine Roman letters bare as sticks.
Now he is older, the birds have no religion.
He walks the industrial gutters that cross the silk routes,
faithful to January, two-faced god of beginnings.
He speaks for, stammers for—mothers, mothers
and mothers, he gets tangled in five thousand years
of apron strings of the Hittite, Greek, Roman,
Christian mother Goddesses and ordinary
women who do most of the work.

He has come to a bridge, the tongue of a balance
that crosses the Bosphorus between Europe
and Asia. He says: "Although it seems for commerce
not wisdom, a br-br-br-br-bridge
across the meandering Bosphorus is a Goddess.
They fa-fa-fa-found her statue near Ephesus."
Her face had a beauty exceptional
even for a God—lady of wild things,
sister of Apollo, from her neck she wore

a wreath of eighteen bull's balls to show
the fear and love the Greeks had for her,
the kind of sacrifice she commanded.

2.

In the agora of rusty girders and broken concrete
sheep graze among burning automobile tires.
At dawn, when Gods roll over in our human beds
and the sea mends the torn robes of the mother Goddess,
in mosques that were churches in Byzantium,
beneath the giant calligraphy of sacred names,
men without shoes, standing,
cup their hands behind their ears at the beginning
of prayer to better hear a voice before they touch
their foreheads to the ground, prostrate themselves.
Strengthened by years of his hatred, and hatred of hatred,
he says, stammering, "They are all covered with dust,
a kind of bone meal of those they have prayed to kill,
hoping to follow the green bird that leads to paradise."

3.

He offers two souls, East and West, over coffee
like honey cakes to Moslems, Christians and Jews.
He writes his love poems in a fifteen-syllable
Greek line. Sweet-faced, bearded, sometimes jailed,
lonely Ottoman of extra syllables,
he sees downhill above the dark river
long accustomed to slaughter,
the marble fragments of ancient tombstones,
the Jewish cemetery, an avalanche of broken writing.
Of course chaos is not separate from form,

not Istanbul nor the exploding suns,
nor is the embroidered slipper
on the foot of the Asian night.
With only his tongue to know, he stammers,
"I leave the lie-the lie-the-lie the likeness to you.
Words come without human intervention:
a word is a sacrificial goat
and the goat sent into the wilderness.
My semen is turned to blood."

DAYDREAM

In a daydream near the lake in Canada,
to save my dog, I fired a shotgun at a bear's head,
turning its face and eyes into bleeding peach pits.
Mama bear gasped something less than a syllable,
made for the forest like a shot,
stood up for a moment at the brambles
like my small son standing in bed asking "Why? Why?"
What can she teach her two cubs now? They are still hungry.
Not the lesson of acorns, not the song of grubs in damp stumps—
that mice are sweet. Once she nursed her cubs while she slept
two heartbeats per minute, under branches and fresh snow.
Now they tongue the blood from her face—
then they die in my cruel song.

FOOL

The first days of March,
the smell of the newborn in the air
brought his guffaws and imitations,
the miracles and illusions of everyday life:
birth, death, love and art as hippopotami
chewing the same grasses, breaking the same wind.
Not myth, not document or hymn,
but a way of laughing by writing
and re-writing; as it turned out he wrote
a farce about the distance between fathers
and sons, mothers and daughters,
who reflect one another, meet
or touch like water and sky
that only seem to touch at a distance.
In a garden under grape leaves,
he rested his head on books and wrote a bad comedy
about the seasons passing more quickly
and the worship and praise his god had disregarded.
He wrote scripture on the inner surface of a bowl,
poured water in, stirred until the writing was dissolved,
then filled his mouth, gargled, swallowed and grinned.

THE HAWK, THE SERPENTS AND THE CLOUD

In writing, he moved from the word *I,*
the word once a serpent curled between the rocks,
to *he,* the word once a hawk drifting above the reeds,
back to *we:* a nest of serpents.
Of course the hawk attacked the serpents.
She became a cloud, nursed us, mothered us,
scrubbed us with rain. *I,* once a serpent, know the Chinese
character for *he* is a standing figure,
the sign for *she* is a kneeling figure,
the word *cloud* is formed by two horizontal waves above a plain,
and that in writing Chinese
you must show feeling for different parts of the word.
Writing contains painting and painting writing.
Each is bird and sky to the other, soil and flower.

LULLABY FOR TWINS

Sleep now little son, little daughter,
so young you have not yet smiled,
your penis and vagina have not yet
been filled with laughter.
You are helpless and wild.
It will come, the look of a smile,
the smile, the laughter,
the playing in bed and water,
your first devotion.
Sleep now on your mother's breast.
It will come a little after—
the sadness under the coverlet,
the plunge into the ocean,
the laughter.

LETTER TO NOAH

Greetings, I hope you will not be disappointed to learn I survived
the flood riding the back of a giant turtle for a year.
Adrift in the waters of chaos, above the ice-covered mountain ranges
that had become part of the deep,
I saw the sun and moon embrace each other in terror.
I kept my senses counting the days that had no name,
I heard all manner of newborn things
crying for their mothers—the last living sounds.
I think I saw the north wind abduct a woman.
We swam through islands of angry faces, an ocean of rodents
devouring each other, great serpents of children knotted
together in whirlpools. I saw the beauty of jungle birds
that in mid-afternoon filled the horizon like a sunset—
once, your vainglorious ark, three stories of lights,
your windows filled with the riches of the world,
a woman on the deck, her wet blouse
clinging to her breasts—I was that close.
If you had heard my call and saw me alive,
would you have reached down to save me?
It wouldn't have been the end of the world.
But you of course were just following orders, a tune as old
as Adam's song to Eve before the serpent.
Then after all the days of night I heard my turtle gasp, "Hallelujah."
I turned and saw the rainbow, the raven and the dove,
in sunlight the waters that reflected nothing, receding,
Noah, I think I am as grateful for the rainbow as you.
I am present, I have survived, corrupt and unclean.

NEW MOON

Full of the city and accounting, I stepped out of my car
into the mist and sand near the Atlantic,
to see a bright haze within a cloud,
a wordless passage from an older testament.
I had forgotten in the unreadable night
that once like a child learning to speak I tried to write,
on a dark night of my life, something lunar,
to be my own Ordinary of secrets and rebirth.
Now the sacred gift of greeting is devoured.

In my silent Holy books I find, after the blessings
called "The Giving Thanks for Trees Blossoming"
and "The Giving Thanks for Fragrance,"
prayers for the new moon in large type,
night prayers for unconscious sins and new beginnings,
to be read outside in moonlight or at an open window.
I speak of prayer, it is not prayer.
I count syllables like minutes before sunset.
I have nothing to show the new moon
but a few lines about the present,
the lesser time under the sun.
Old enough, I have learned to be my own child:
I carry myself on my shoulders, whipping and laughing.
To get even, have I lived my life to make adults cry?
Tonight the child runs to and from me,
already full of memory and cruel history,
talking a blue streak about injustices.
The child falls asleep. I'm up late with the moon.
It is not revelation but the mystery itself I praise.

THE MISCARRIAGE

1.

You had almost no time, you were something
not quite penciled in, you were more than darkness
that is shaped by its being and its distance from light.
(To give birth in Spanish is to give to light.)
There was the poetry of it:
a word, a letter changed perhaps
or missing and you were gone.
Every word is changed when spoken.
The beauty is you were mine and hers,
not like a house, a bed, a book or a dog,
unsellable, unreadable, not love, but of love,
an of—with a certain roundness and a speck
that might have become an eye, might have
seen something, anything: light,
Tuscany, Montana, read Homer in Greek—
unnamed of, saved from light and darkness.

2.

I was not told of you until long after,
I would not have handed down that suitcase
to her through the train window in Florence
had I known. I might have suggested tea
instead of *Strega*, might have fanned the air.
Fathers can do something. I didn't ask the right questions.
I did not offer any sacrifice.
I just walked around in my usual fog looking
at pictures of the Virgin impregnated by words.

What if the Virgin Mother had miscarried? What if
the Magi arrived with all that myrrh and frankincense
like dinner guests on the wrong evening.
Our Lady embarrassed, straightening up,
Joseph offering them chairs he made and a little wine,
sinners stoned in the street
while John who would have been called the Baptist
wept in his mother's belly.

POSTCARD TO WALT WHITMAN FROM SIENA

Today the windy Italian air was clean as the air of Montauk,
I walked through a huge vaulted hall,
a Renaissance hospital opposite the Duomo,
and I thought of you in your forties,
writing letters for the wounded and dying—
to nurse the horribly wounded,
you did not need to think of them as Jesus.
In the dark galleries, a kind of gossip
about the life of Christ,
the paintings are "gold ground,"
gold leaf, not leaves of grass. The painters
worked for the honor of illumination,
did not sign their work that was a form of prayer—
a signature can deflower a lily.
I saw a cradle that was a cathedral rocking,
I remembered you sang Italian arias
and the Star-Spangled Banner in your bathtub.
At five o'clock I heard the rosary,
the *joys* and *sorrows* of the Virgin,
had a café latte, then returned to hear the litany:
"star of the sea, lily of the valley, tower of ivory"—
something like you praising America.

PANDA SONG

I hear the panda's song,
on lonely afternoons
he strips bamboo with a false thumb,
uooh, uooh,
an inefficient contraption, part of his wrist,
while his real thumb is committed,
uooh, uooh,
for evolutionary and historical reasons,
to other work, mostly running and clawing,
uooh.

Neither lover nor patriot, there is a cricket,
err, err,
that left in Puerto Rico
lives out its days,
err,
that dies if moved
off its sugarcane island
to Santo Domingo, Curaçao or Florida.
Err......uooh, uooh,
small matters the law does not correct,
uooh, err, err.

A GAMBLER'S STORY

There was a risk, a dividing of waters,
there was an Irish Jew whose father arrived
in Belfast from Kovno, heard English,
got off the boat and was in Ireland three years
before he discovered he wasn't in England.
A revolutionary with a darling Irish accent,
the son, a family man, seduced his father's mistress
and his brother's wife, lost the money for a rainy day,
then their daily bread. My friend vanished for a year,
returned with his winnings, scrounged for years
till he won £100,000 at baccarat,
which he gave to his wife and children—
then disappeared in Provence. Still on a roll, he studied
mystical philosophy, the greatest of crapshoots:
the earth winning the familiar waters,
the stars taking the heavens, darkness the big winner.
He borrowed money from me and others
when we needed it—never paid it back.

JUDAS

Judas, red-haired patron saint of bankers,
I run an internal revenue service, audit me.
For my losses carried forward more than a half century,
allow only the last five years as deduction.
Call my write-off for European travel
and business entertainment, mere pleasure trips.
There is a difference between writing, rewriting
and cooking the books. Accounting in the dark
I have mortgaged more than my house,
my heart pays usurious interest.
To whom is such a price paid, to what treasury?
Judas, your God with his small coins
of good and evil lends Himself to fictions.
I am in the market for bracelets,
chains, necklaces and rings of illumination.

THE PROOF

To Arnold Cooper

It comes down to this: I saw the room a little tilted
and you saw it straight, and when you proved it with a ruler
and leveler I fought back: "The ruler might be wrong,
no inch is equal to any other inch. There are no equal numbers,
there is just an agreement as to what they mean.
I pity the violinist who just plays the notes.
The roof of your house is not a sonata,
or an apple tree a violin, whoever plucks the fruit."
And worse, you, old friend, know better than I
the uniqueness of human beings,
you measured hoping to prove me right.
Once when we caught a stringer full of bass,
I tied them to an oarlock with my best knot
that slipped—our fish disappeared.
You forgave me with an archaic smile.
We are the same age, equals before the law,
but one will slip away under the waterlilies
before the other. Whoever slips away first,
proving me right about the ceiling, the roof and inches—
the other shall hold a kind of grudge.

THREE MARYS

In Spain I took a yellow cab up Jew Mountain
to a Golgotha of telephone poles,
I saw a horizon of lovers
suffering a hundred different deaths,
I saw time as a mother in the lap of her mother,
kiss, give suck as women do in the beginning
—their hands made the wetness they touched.
I had them both and a Magdalene.

Three Marys, O what confusion!
I went into time and women like entering a cathedral:
Was, Is and Will Be as if they were eternal.
Madness to think sweating beauty needed me.
Above me, higher than the darkness,
stained glass windows told another story:
the speaking of the flesh, the *parlando*, the *hablar*.

What have women taught me, my beautiful teachers,
after all that lovemaking, that bathing?
How to read, dress and keep clean. Sweet one,
it is time to take on the inconveniences,
time to make and repair,
ways of kindness and deception,
ways to go to funerals and weddings—
toujours la tendresse.

2.

It's a spring day near the Atlantic—
the sky as blue as her eyes,
time undresses before me,
moves like a girl
lifting her blouse over her head.

Now the quarrel really begins:
I tell her I have no complaints so far,
I'm not really speaking for myself—
that I don't want her to go.
I've seen the suffering she caused her lovers,
their utter humiliation.
Yes, old men and young boys,
old women and young girls.

Naked, she takes a mouthful of wine—
smiling her wicked rose-petal smile,
her eyes an endless intelligent blue,
she leans over me and from above
pushes the wine into my mouth—
then puts her hand to my lips
as if to tell me
I was saying the wrong thing.

AMPHORA

They will keep his ashes
in a Greek red and black figured pot,
side A: a temple to Dionysus,
side B: a man of little fame is sailing alone in a boat
that is a great red and black figured prick.
He is singing.
The boat sinks its prow into the foaming sea.

ON TRYING TO REMEMBER
TWO CHINESE POEMS

1.

I've forgotten the book, the poet,
the beauty of calligraphy,
the poems made to be seen and read out loud,
two lost songs on hanging scrolls
stolen by foreigners . . .

2.

White as frost,
a piece of freshly woven silk
made a fan, a bright moon.
She, or my lady, kept a fan nearby,
its motion a gentle summer breeze
. . . he dreaded the coming of autumn
when the north wind breaks the summer heat
and the fan is dropped unwanted
into a lacquer box,
its short term of favor ended.

3.

A catalog of beds:
riverbed, flower bed, family bed.
My mother died when I was three,
dreadful to be a child in baby clothes.
I climbed into her bed and tried to nurse,

clutching her body with all my strength;
not knowing she was dead I spoke to her,
called to her. I remember thinking,
before, when I wept and ached for her,
although she was sick she came to me,
she whispered and caressed me,
then the lamp went out
and my mother coughed by the chilly window.

4.

...A night of restless birds.
Without warning
a great forest fire, a devouring flaming wind,
rolling mountains of fire
with nothing to stop them but the sea.
Woman is half the sky.

APRIL, BEIJING

Some of the self-containment of my old face
has been sand-blasted away. The "yellow wind"
is blowing and my mouth and face burn
from the Gobi dust that scorches the city
after its historic passage over the Great Wall.
When I was young, I hosed the Atlantic salt
off my body—the salt was young too.

In China, "ashes to ashes and dust to dust"
means something more; work, no matter how cruel,
is part prophecy. Workers in fields
that were Chinese eight thousand years ago,
their plows and terraces a kind of calligraphy,
face the living and the dead, whose windy fortress
takes on a mortal form: the Great Wall.
Even here the North Wind abducts a beauty.
Never before have I heard ancient laughter.
In China, I can taste the dust on my own grave
like salt. The winter coal dust shadows every wall
and window, darkens the lattice and the rose,
offers its gray society to the blue cornflower,
the saffron crocus, the red poppy.

                    The moon
brushed by calligraphy, poetry and clouds,
touched, lowered toward mortality—
to silk, to chess, to science, to paper,
requires that the word and painting respond
more intimately to each other, when the heart
is loneliest and in need of a mother,
when the ocean is drifting away,

when the mountains seem further off.
The birds sing in the dark before sunrise
because sunlight is delayed by dust and the sound
of a poet grinding his own ink from stone
according to the moon's teaching.
I am happy to be here, even if I can't breathe.
The emperor of time falls from a tree,
the dust rises.

CHINA SONNET

On a red banner across the center of this poem
there is painted in gold Chinese letters:
"Strive to Build Socialist Spiritual Civilization."
On the right side hangs a red banner saying,
"Intellectuals: Cleaning Shithouses for Ten Years
in the Cultural Revolution Clears the Head."
Down the left side is pasted
a lantern-thin red and black paper-saying,
"When Spring Comes Back, the Earth is Green."
Off the page is China: the people give little importance
to what they call "spring couplets," the paper-sayings
pasted with wheat-flour and water above the lintels
and down the sills of peasant houses. They seldom notice
they enter and depart through the doors of poetry.

WALKING

1.

His stride is part delusion.
They laugh at him, "A little water in the boot,
he thinks he walks on water."
At home to get a cup of coffee
he walks across Norway, and his talk—
he speaks intimately to crowds,
and to one as a crowd. On principle
he never eats small potatoes.
Illusion, mirage, hallucination,
he loves a night painting of a fable: a man
is grinning at a boy lighting a candle from an ember,
a monkey, on his shoulder, chained to heaven—
a reminder that art apes nature.
When they told him reality is simply what is,
it was as though he had climbed Sinai,
then walked down to get the laws.
He dreams only of the migrations of peoples
beneath the migrations of birds,
he wakes to new nations, he yawns
riddles of the north and south wind,
whistles his own tune in the holy sepulchre.
Some afternoons he stretches out in a field
like an aqueduct, "All we do," he says,
"is carry a bucket or two of God's waters
from place to place."

2.

Under a roof, and in the open air,
hangs an amusing tragedy, a kind of satyr play,
but not every fat man dancing by
is wrapped in grape leaves. Facing himself
in an old brass mirror like the one
the ancient Chinese thought cured insanity,
tongue-tied he speaks to his own secret face,
or standing in the sunlight
against the lives of mountains, sky and sea,
he speaks, made-up and masked, the lyrical truth,
the bare-faced lie.
Not speaking the language of his fathers,
a hero may die because all flesh is grass
and he forgets the password.

From a lectern, or the top of a hay wagon,
or leaping down,
a few steps away from everyday life,
into something like a kitchen garden
he unearths in the wordless soil
things sung or said, kinds of meaning:
what is denoted or symbolic,
or understood only by its music,
or caught onto without reason,
the endless twisting of its roots, its clarity—
aware of the old meaning of looking
to the Last Judgment,
that nothing is merely or only.

3.

At a garden party he almost said,
"Madame, it is not in the bones of a lover or a dog
to wait as long as the bleached mollusk shell
on the mountain. Time is an ice cube melting
in a bowl, the world is refracted, ridiculous.
In life, you often reach out for a stone
that isn't where you see it in the stream."
But it was summer,
no one would believe time was so cold
on a hot day, so comforting,
when the purple iris was already dry
and the tulips fallen.

THE DEBT

1.

I owe a debt to the night,
I must pay it back, darkness for darkness
plus interest.
I must make something out of almost nothing,
I can't pay back by just not sleeping
night after night. I hear them screaming
in the streets of New York, "What? What? What?"

I can't write a check to the night,
or a promissory note: "I'll write songs."
Only the nightmare is legal tender.
I bribe owls, I appeal
to creatures of the night: "Help me
raccoons, catfish, snakes!"
I put my head in the tunnel of a raccoon,
pick up a fish spine in my mouth.
Perhaps the night will accept this?
Dying is my only asset.

These days driving along I turn up my brights.
I love and am grateful for anything that lights
the darkness: matches, fireworks, fireflies.
My friend who's been to Antarctica
tells me when the sun is high against the ice
you see the shadow of the earth.
The night after all is just a shadow. . .
The debt keeps mounting.
I try to repay something by remembering
my Dante, the old five and ten thousand lira notes

had Dante's face etched on the front.
(I bought that cheap.) Hard cash to the night
is finding out what I do not want to know
about myself, no facts acceptable,
a passage through darkness,
where the one I stop to ask "Why? What?"
is always myself, I cannot recognize.

2.

If only I could coin nightmares:
a barnyard in Asia,
the last dog and cat betrayed, are no more.
A small herd of three-legged blind cows
still gives milk.
A pig with a missing snout, its face like a moon,
wades in a brook.
A horse, its mane burnt to cinders,
a rear hip socket shot off, tries to get up,
thrusting its muzzle into the dark grass.
A rooster pecks without a beak or a coxcomb.
A rabbit that eats stones, sips without a tongue,
runs without feet.
A ditch of goats, sheep and oxen
locked in some kind of embrace.
All move their faces away,
refuse the charity of man
the warrior, the domesticator.
I see a whale with eyes yards apart
swimming out of the horizon,
surfacing as if it were going to die,
with a last disassociated vision,
one eye at peace
peers down into the valleys and mountains

of the ocean, the other eye floats,
tries to talk with its lids to the multitude.
While in the great head
what is happening and what happened mingle,
for neither has to be.
I pray for some of my eyes to open and some to close.
It is the night itself that provides
a forgiveness.

3

poems from

SKULL OF ADAM (1979)

&

THE WRONG ANGEL (1966)

ON SEEING AN X-RAY OF MY HEAD

This face without race or religion,
I have in common with humanity—
Mouth without lips, jaws without tongue,
this face does not sleep when I sleep,
gives no hint of love or pleasure,
my most recent portrait smells of fixative
and rancid vinegar, does not appear
male or female.
I don't look as if I work for a living.

I will ask for fire. I can't risk
lovers, walking in a wood, turning this face,
seeing such putrefaction they question
why they've come to lie on the grass,
picnic, fish or read to one another.
I will not have them find me staring
after their lovemaking—
under the leaves and branches of summer,
a reminder of mortality.

I prefer the good life, in real death
a useful skull to house small fish
or strawberries, a little company.
I must remember death is not always
a humiliation, life everlasting
is to be loved at the moment of death.
I hold my lantern head before me,
peer into one eye, see darkness, darkness
in the other, great funerals of darkness
that never meet.

UNCERTAIN WEATHER

Uncertain weather.
The most aloof birds
come closer to the earth,
confused by the apparent
lowering of the clouds and sky.
I walk in these descending clouds.
Gulls set off
The fish don't care
I surf-cast a silver spoon
into the clouds
in the direction of the sea.

Last summer in Long Island
I saw a pair of white egrets
standing at the shoreline.
Now in Jamaica
I see hundreds swooping above me,
beyond Fern Gully
where the roads lead into fields of sugar cane,
the old slave plantations.

The flights of egrets remind me
of alarmed swallows—
then I see what they are doing:
hundreds of white birds
are trying to drive
a single buzzard out of the valley,
diving again and again to protect their nests.
In just a few days
I have become accustomed

164

to seeing egrets perched on cattle
or standing beside, motionless.
Now I see them fighting for life,
summoning whatever violence they have,
unable to be graceless.
One by one, not as a flock,
the birds dive, pursue,
do not touch.
Off the Caribbean,
a fresh afternoon wind
lifts the egrets higher
and gives the red-throated scavenger,
who must also feed its young,
a momentary passage
down into the tall moist grass.

BLACK DOG

I fly the flag of the menstruating black dog:
a black dog dripping blood over us all.
My flag barks, licks my face,
my flag says, "I am alive, willing,
part of the natural order of things.
You are a supernatural creature."

I walk across the road to the stream.
In a rush of water—something surfaces:
a snake has caught a trout by the anus,
lifts the fish out of the water—I hold my dog back.
The snake's head cuts a line through the shaded stream
into the sunlight,
crosses the water to a ledge of gravel and jewelweed.
The trout is held into the summer air,
its brightest colors already begun to fade.
The snake swallows the fish headfirst.

A tree, remembering my mother, kisses me;
why shouldn't I love to sleep at the foot of a tree,
she taught me to kiss the sweet dog who licks
the face of a bum passed out in the park.
I salute the flag of my dog sprawled on the floor
of all-night restaurants. My dog pledges allegiance,
stands up and barks because the entire shape of time
is a greater, more ferocious beast than anything in it.

THE MEETING

It took me some seconds as I drove toward
the white pillowcase, or was it a towel
blowing across the road, to see what it was.
In Long Island near sanctuaries
where there are still geese and swans,
I thought a swan was hit by an automobile.
I was afraid to hurt it. The beautiful creature
rolled in sensual agony,
then reached out to attack me.
Why do I feel something happened on the road,
a transfiguration, a transgression,
as if I hadn't come to see what was,
but confronted the white body,
tried to lift, help her fly,
or slit its throat.
Why did I need this illusion,
a beauty lying helpless?

THE IMPROVEMENT

Since they were morose in August,
not worth saving,
I paid to have the junipers torn out
trunk and root; the roots had enough strength
to pull the truck back down so hard
the wheels broke the brick walk.

Heaped in front of my house
green and dry gray branches
that did not suffer
but had beauty to lose.
Rather than have the branches dumped or burned,
I dragged them to the bulkhead
and pushed them into the bay.

Damp roots, what do I know
of the tenderness of earth,
the girlish blonde dust?

POTATO SONG

Darkness, sunlight and a little holy spit
don't explain an onion with its rose windows
and presentiment of the sublime,
a green shoot growing out of rock
or the endless farewells of trees.
Wild grasses don't grow just to feed sheep,
hold down the soil or keep stones from rolling;
they're meant to be seen, give joy, break the heart.
But potatoes hardly have a way of knowing.
They sense if it is raining or not,
how much sunlight or darkness they have,
not which wind is blowing or if there are dark clouds
or red-winged blackbirds overhead.
They are not aware if there are soldiers in the field
or not, moles or underground humpings.
Potatoes do not sleep, but must find pleasure
in their flowering. Sometimes
I hear them call me "mister" from the ditch.
Workers outside my window in Long Island
cut potatoes in pieces, bury them, water them.
Each part is likely to sprout and flower.
No one so lordly as not to envy that.

FISHING IN THE EVENING

In late September on a school day
I take my father, failing, now past seventy
to the rowboat on the reservoir; the waters
since July have gone down two hundred yards
below the shoreline.
The lake stretches before us—a secret,
we do not disturb a drifting branch, a single hawk.
For a moment nothing says, "thou shalt not."
If I could say anything to the sky and trees
I'd say things are best as they are.

It is more difficult for me to think
of my father's death than my own.
He casts half the distance he used to.
I am trying to give him something,
to stuff a hill between his lips.
I try to spoon-feed him nature, but an hour
in the evening on the lake doesn't nourish him;
the walk in the woods that comforts me
as it used to comfort him makes him shiver.
I pretend to be cold.

We walk back along the drying lake bottom,
our shoes sink into the cold mud—
where last spring there were ten feet of water,
where in early June I saw golden carp
coupling on the surface. It's after dark,
although I can barely see
I think I know where the fence is.
My father's hands tremble like the tail of a fish
resting in one place. As for me?
I have already become his ghost.

170

PRAYER

Give me a death like Buddha's. Let me fall
over from eating mushrooms Provençale,
a peasant wine pouring down my shirt-front,
my last request not a cry but a grunt.
Kicking my heels to heaven, may I succumb
tumbling into a rosebush after a love
half my age. Though I'm deposed, my tomb
shall not be empty; may my belly show above
my coffin like a distant hill, my mourners come
as if to pass an hour in the country,
to see the green, that old anarchy.

A SKETCH OF SLAVES,
JEWS IN CONCENTRATION CAMPS
AND UNHAPPY LOVERS

The survivors have something in common—
captured by superior forces of violence,
probably in the middle of the night,
dumped into slave ship, boxcar or bed,
the smell of urine and feces in their nostrils,
the useless are directed by a finger
to the right, the useful to the left—
examined naked. They cannot worship
their own Gods or the Gods of their masters.
The "old-timers" become like children, they steal,
inform, giggle, learn to seem not there,
not to do anything extraordinary
like whistling or talking. They grow proud
of how smartly they stand at attention;
finally some come to believe the rules
set down from above are desirable,
at least in camp or bed. A few climb for air
on the bodies of others, dig their fingernails
into the plaster ceiling, trying to escape
the suffocation. I thumb through the naked corpses
for my hidden life. You who are free,
relax, your stomachs will soon settle.
Isn't it May? Aren't you happy as larks?

KANGAROO

My soul climbs up my legs,
buries its face in blood and veins,
locks its jaws on the nipple that is me.
I jump my way into the desert.
What does my soul, safe in its pocket, care
what I say to desert flowers?
Like a kangaroo
I pray and mock prayer.

I never took a vow of darkness.
I sit beside a boulder writing
on yellow lined paper. Once I thought
I'll pull my soul out of my mouth,
a lion will sleep at my feet,
I'll spend forty days in the desert,
I'll find something remarkable, a sign:
strains of desert grass
send the root of a single blade
down thirty feet.
I remember flakes of dry blood,
the incredible rescue of the man by the soul.

Under the aching knuckles of the wind,
move down in your pocket
away from remorse and money.
Learn discomfort from the frog,
the worm, the gliding crow,
they all hunt in repose, like men in prayer.
I can hardly distinguish myself from darkness.
I am not what I am. I demand the heart
to answer for what is given. I jump into the desert,
a big Jew, the law under my arm like bread.

THE RETURN

It was justice to see her nude haunches
backing toward me again after the years,
familiar as water after long thirst.
Now like a stream she is, and I can lie beside
running my hand over the waters, or sleep;
but the water is colder, the gullies darker,
the rapids that threw me down have shallowed;
I can walk across.

THE GIFT

She has given me the gift of my own desire;
Hollowed by fire as a tree
I have betrayed love and desire.

Gladly I would betray desire
But I cannot, until once more
Love burns me through.

POEM BEFORE MARRIAGE

I am part man, part seagull, part turtle.
What remains? I have a few seasons
of vanity and forty years in the muddy lake.
I float on the reservoir in Central Park,
my gull eyes, man flesh, turtle mouth, tear the water
hunting shadows of fish that never appear.
I live on things a great city
puts in a small bowl for emergencies.
I "Caw Caw," wishing the shell on my back
were a musical instrument.
I have already been picked out of the mud
three times and thrown
against apartment house walls, left for dead.

Jane, in my bed you will find feathers
and fragments of shell. When, swallowing darkness,
I have a nightmare in your arms, my eyes
film over, let me sink to the bottom
of the artificial lake.

Fish for me.

LOVERS

We are gravel in the riverbed.
Years set us together in a bed of clay.
The river passes over us like suffering,
spring rains wash out the pine saplings,
in loneliness great trees sweep downstream—
avalanche, falling shale, water becomes mud,
becomes rock, willows root, startled trout
rest and spawn upon us,
a fisherman may push his boot
into our throats.

We know there are mountains:
we see them above the waters
as a single purple, blue and white blossom.
The river has changed course, leaving its bed.
What can I bring you,
facing the moon and the mountain?
We are used to seeing water,
then the moonlight on the surface of the water,
then the night, finally the moon itself.
The world comes, offers bread and fish
not stone and serpent.

THE VALLEY

Once I was jealous of lovers.
Now I am jealous of things that outlast us—
the road between Route 28 and our house,
the bridge over the river,
a valley of second growth trees.
Under the birches, vines
the color of wolves survive a winter ten below,
while the unpicked apples turn black
and the picked fruit is red in the basket.
I am not sure that the hand of God
and the hand of man ever touch,
even by chance.

JANE'S GRANDMOTHER

Light as a sparrow
she sits on a burnished leather davenport,
the kind you can't slump in.
Near her 104th year, her death is almost lost
like the comb that keeps her hair in place.
The rivers are older than she is.
In Montana the clouds are younger than she is—
there's not much standing between anything
and the sky—the darkness older,
some trees older, the great withstanders.
The barbed wire runs from U.S. 6
into her fingers and arms.
Her daughters care for her fingernails,
brown shell of box turtle.
Honest homesteader, she still loves a kiss.
Her smile moves to the rings of a tree,
her daughters' faces and their daughters'.

FROG

I hold this living coldness,
this gland with eyes, mouth, feet,
shattered mirror of all creatures,
pulsing smile of fish, serpent and man,
feet and hands come out of a head
that is also a tail,
just as I caught him most of my life ago
in the sawdust of the icehouse.
I could not believe in him if he were not here.
He rests my spirit
and is beautiful as waterlilies.
The sound of his call is too large for his body:
"irrelevant, irrelevant, irrelevant."
Once in the dry countries he was a god.

APOCRYPHA

You lie in my arms,
sunlight fills the abandoned quarries.
I planted five Lombard poplars,
two apple trees died of my error,
three others should be doing better.
I prepared the soil,
I painted over the diseased apple tree,
I buried the available dead around it:
thirty trout that died in the pond
when I tried to kill the algae, a run-over raccoon,
a hive of maggots in every hole.
This year the tree flowered, bears fruit.
Are my cures temporary?

I chose abortion in place of a son,
because of considerations.
I look for the abandoned dead,
the victims; I shall wash them,
trim their fingernails and toenails.
I learn to say Kaddish,
to speak its Hebrew correctly,
a language I do not know,
should I be called upon.
I abandon flesh of my flesh
for a life of my choosing.

I take my life from Apocrypha.
Warning of the destruction of the city,
I send away the angel Raphael
and my son. Not knowing if I am right
or wrong, I fall asleep in the garden,

I am blinded by the droppings
of a hummingbird or crow.
Will my son wash my eyes with fish gall
restoring my sight?

Go in darkness, mouth to mouth
is the command.
I kiss the book,
not wanting to speak
of the suffering I have caused.
Sacred and defiled,
my soul is right
to deal with me in secret.

MORNING

Why does she pick only the smallest wild flowers?
The daisy and day lily aren't gross,
lilacs, peonies and roses
are not base company.
Why are they so small, the wild flowers
she brings me,
the most delicate, purest of color?
What is their purpose,
brought by her hand to the hand of her lover?

Usually I wake
to a dreamlike landscape,
face outside my window—
the Atlantic, a Catskill stream,
or the lake in Central Park.
My breath stares,
my tongue regards,
I whisper in my wife's ear,
"Are you up?"
Some voices can see,
some see for others, change the world.
All my voice can do is sleep near her ear,
while she chooses to sleep or wake.

OLD

The turtles are out,
loners on the road listening for mud,
old people looking for money.
Father, too old for hope,
when trees are burned black with cold,
what belongs to man, and what to nature?

With a penknife you used to make
ashtrays of turtles,
scrape out the living flesh
gifts for friends,
now mine to take home if I want to.
A shell of your old self,
I want to whisper to you
the prayers and psalms you never taught me.
I never learned a healthy disrespect.
On my table I keep a bronze turtle—
a handle torn from an African sword,
a symbol of destroyed power.

The turtles move under the snow
in the dead of winter, under the loam,
chewing and scratching into frozen sand,
deeper than moles or grubs,
far from the loneliness of sunlight and weather.
I offer my hand, a strange other element.

PHOTOGRAPHY ISN'T ART

1.

If I gave up the camera
or really made myself into a camera
or into a photograph,
if the sight of that photograph
made me change my life,
if I really held my darkest self
up to the light,
where life cannot be violated
by enlargers, light meters—
what creature would such changes keep alive?

My work changes color because of the work
like the hands of people handling coins.
The pregnant black woman
I saw during the blackout in New York City
carrying a refrigerator on her back
was not only a likeness.
Visions hide more than they reveal.

2.

If I could really become a blur,
if I became for the joy of it—say a photograph
taken in a forgiving light
of the guests seated around the table
at Delacroix's dinner party, Paris, 1857,
when he had just made an omelette

so beautiful no one would eat it—
then if they called me to join at table
that company of poets and painters,
I would sweep the skull of Adam off the cloth,
smile for the photographer,
give thanks and suggest
we eat the omelette while it's still hot.

NICKY

She danced into the moonless winter,
a black dog.
In the morning when I found her
I couldn't get her tongue back in her mouth.
She lies between a Japanese maple
and the cellar door, at no one's feet,
without a master.

WAR BALLAD

(after the Russian)

The piano has crawled into the quarry. Hauled
In last night for firewood, sprawled
With frozen barrels, crates and sticks,
The piano is waiting for the axe.

Legless, a black box, still polished;
It lies on its belly like a lizard,
Droning, heaving, hardly fashioned
For the quarry's primordial art.

Blood red: his frozen fingers cleft,
Two on the right hand, five on the left,
He goes down on his knees to reach the keyboard,
To strike the lizard's chord.

Seven fingers pick out rhymes and rhythm,
The frozen skin, steaming, peels off them,
As from a boiled potato. Their schemes,
Their beauty, ivory and anthracite,
Flicker and flash like the great Northern Lights.

Everything played before is a great lie.
The reflections of flaming chandeliers—
Deceit, the white columns, the grand tiers
In warm concert halls—wild lies.

But the steel of the piano howls in me,
I lie in the quarry and I am deft
As the lizard. I accept the gift.
I'll be a song for Russia, I'll be
an étude, warmth and bread for everybody.

188

VOMIT

The stomach and the heart can be torn
out through the mouth if you get the right hook.
Because puking I was held up to this world,
because I have lived, burped in my mother's arms,
it comes out now:
what I thought I had swallowed, matters settled,
understood, kept out of mind—our father
who keeps us in the speeding car,
who will not stop, let me puke in the grass
where it will hardly be noticed,
among the weeds and roadside flowers.

I throw up on myself the half-digested
meat and salad of what I devoured
in pleasure, the perfectly seasoned
explanation of love and social forces
that made me feel slightly superior.

I put my finger down my throat
so I can become part of this world,
I refuse to hear voices that speak to me
in rage without sense,
because my body and soul are locked
in secret battle, because the soul is voiceless
while the body can speak, gasp, sing, whisper,
utter what it pleases, because the body
becomes what it consumes and the soul
refuses such fires;
because the devil says
vomit is the speech of the soul.

I give the devil his due,
because the soul's speech is so rare,
to hear it
I must listen out of earshot,
I must give myself like a lover
and take like a lover, resisting and giving
till the heart is hooked and pulled out.

SAINT MERDE

I've been taught my daily lesson,
that man shall squat alone in secret,
I've been taken off my high horse,
I've bent down,
interrupted my day to humble myself,
no need to fall on my knees.
With a genuflection of the gut,
I hunt where my bones stink.

Out of the pain of this world
a kindness, a shape each of us
learns by heart: moon crescent,
jewelweed, forget-me-not,
hot lava. Christ, is this
the ghost in everything,
what I can and cannot,
I will and will not,
I have and have not,
what I must and must not,
what I did and did not?
An infant gasps in ecstasy,
tears of shit drip from a man
who cannot cry.

Most men near death cannot withhold,
they shit on themselves
when what they are
is all out of them:
wind, kindness, cruelty
all done, left behind,
when they must be changed
and cannot remember
who chose to soil us,
who makes us clean.

SNOT

I cannot forget the little swamp
that grows in my head,
cousin of the tear,
snot, my lowly, not worthy of sorrow,
the body's only
completely unsexual secretion.
No one my dears is hot for snot
or its institutions: catarrh,
asthma, the common cold, although
I've heard "snot-nose" used to mean "darling"
or "my son." There's beauty in it,
familiar as the face of any friend.
Dogs eat it, no one gets rich on it.

AN EXCHANGE OF HATS

I will my collection of hats,
straw the Yucatan, fez Algiers 1935,
Russian beaver, Irish fisherman's knit,
collapsible silk opera, a Borsalino,
to a dead man,
the Portuguese poet, my dear Fernando,
who, without common loyalty,
wrote under seven different names
in seven different styles.
He was a man of many cafés,
a smoker and non-smoker.
His poets came to live in Lisbon,
had different sexual preferences,
histories and regional accents.

Still their poems had a common smell
and loneliness that was Fernando's.
His own character
was to him like ink to a squid,
something to hide behind.
What did it matter, writing in Portuguese
after the First World War? The center was Paris,
the languages French and English.

In Lisbon, workers on the street corner were arguing
over what was elegance, the anarchist manifesto,
the trial of Captain Artur Carlos de Barros
found guilty of "advocating circumcision"
and teaching Marranos no longer to enter church
saying "When I enter I adore neither wood nor stone
but only the Ancient of Days who rules all."

The Portuguese say
they have the "illusion" to do something,
meaning they very much want to do it.
He could not just sit in the same café
wearing his own last hat, drinking port
and smoking *Ideals* forever.

CLAMS

Ancient of Days, bless the innocent
who can do nothing but cling,
open or close their stone mouths.
Out of water they live on themselves
and what little sea water they carry with them.
Bless all things unaware that perceive
life and death as comfort or discomfort:
bless their great dumbness.

We die misinformed
with our mouths of shell open.
At the last moment, as our lives fall off,
a gull lifts us, drops us on the rocks, bare
because the tide is out. Flesh sifts the sludge.
At sea bottom, on the rocks below the wharf,
a salt foot, too humble to have a voice,
thumps for representation, joy.

LOT'S SON

Three in his arms we sleep, Lot lies awake
All night, he does not let me lie awake
Or cut my own meat. All night
Through my ribs, I feel his body's heat.
He will not let me drink from a bright cup
(Unless he wash it), or climb high up.
His game: he points a finger at my eye
Saying, "You are crying," until I cry,
To make me a man. Rope, he holds me taut,
He knots, undoes the knots, I am caught
Round myself. A knot ties mother to son
Not father to daughter; all rope, but Lot,
Lot who tied us together is undone.

PRAYER FOR AN ACTOR

Señor, already someone else,
O my clown,
the man in your image
was a bestiary,
sweet as sugar,
beautiful as the world,
lizard sitting on a trellis
follows blonde into john,
now he is a butterfly on the edge
of a black-eyed susan
—rhinoceros
filing down his own horn
for aphrodisiac.
Señor, already someone else,
a band of actors under bombardment
played Shakespeare,
the last days
of the Warsaw ghetto,
a few of the survivors
who crawled through the sewers
heard the SS was giving out visas
for America
at a certain hotel,
went to apply.
If you love life
you simply can't believe
how bad it is.
Señor, someone else,
a Yahweh clown,
rectal thermometer of the world,
the tears themselves leave scars.
Farewell art of illusion,
playing yourself as a crowd.

SAILING FROM THE UNITED STATES

In this country I planted not one seed,
Moved from address to address, did not plead
For justice in its courts, fell in love and out,
Thrust my arm into the sea and could not pull it out;
I did not see the summer lose its balance,
Or organize the lonely in a gang, by chance
I did not build a city or a ship, or burn
The leaves that fell last autumn, in my turn
Built by the numb city building noise,
I learned the morning and the night are decoys
To catch a life and heap the profits of the grave.

I have lost a country, its hills and heroes;
In a country that taught me talk, confined
To the city of myself, I oppose
The marketplace and thoroughfares, my mind
Shaping this history, my mouth to zero.
The wind in my house is not a wind through olive trees,
I hear no music in the janitor's keys,
I fashion no reed, no pipe, have not the wind for it,
My summer and winter prove counterfeit.
Through the villages of New England and the free country,
I will my unconditional mutiny,
I leave this crockery heaped on a shelf,
For an old regime, to work myself
As a mine, subject to explosions and cave-in.

PASTORAL

Peace for this poor earth, this plant
Torn out by the wind, this rage,
This world, man's leech that nursed him
Into light; the rivers flood a wreckage
Of soldiers on our common farm,
In whose eyes weeping
We see the dead cheaply,
While naked earth steals naked to our arms,
And the fish can hardly keep from leaping.

WINTER IN VERMONT

Where is the green, the revolutionary?
What good can come of snow and slate?
Vermont or father, what's my theme?
I eye the skin of a woodchuck
Left hanging on barbed wire.
A stream moves under a foot of ice
Like the last words of Henry Adams:
"My child, keep me alive."

THE HANGMAN'S LOVE SONG

In the house of the hangman
do not talk of rope,
or use death, half death,
little death; the victim
always hangs himself,
trap sprung, tongue ripped
like love in the house.
Despite the world's
regalia, I want
a useful funeral.
High, on tiptoe,
swinging back
and forth, the victim,
who cannot speak,
mimics the bell,
such things as bait
for wild game, and love.
Brain hung and heart,
hope swings, sun creaks,
rope in the wind,
and the hangman sings.

CASTELLO DI SERMONETTA

1.

You could only be in Italy;
Beyond the windows cornered with marble roses
A villager carved for a Borgia Pope,
Above the tower thrust up to a stone sky,
An old falcon the color of the walls,
Whose race adapts most easily to castles,
Half blind and alone, chases
An imaginary field mouse across Latina.

2.

Nothing that was saved remains:
A dog in the courtyard too old to bark,
An iron bridge shadows the roots of olive trees,
Betrayed, a cat in the moat licks itself.
Chains that rotted heretic and slave bone
Gossip now of archangels and martyrs,
A headless angel
Sings with collars of bees around his throat,
Three kingless donkeys stray on a hill.
Every man's back breaks.

3.

Down a tower passage
I follow a Gregorian summer,
Savior of insects, to a Christ scraped on a wall
By a boot nail,
Flies humming about in search of a carcass.

Scraped on the wall I see some Liberty:
"January one fifteen-thirty-one
They took the irons off my feet."

Old guests and old hosts in hell and paradise.

ALONG THE TIBER: A COMMENTARY

ANTONY WITH CLEOPATRA

Certainly our fields were planted
With lilac and poppies
When there was need of cotton and wheat.
So toward the end of summer
We began our walks on the outskirts of the city
To watch for the coming of strangers.

We were not young—but excellent.
What a long way from Italy,
The Nile never seemed so deep;
It was the very brim of summer,
Still the best time of the year for love,
Roman soldiers dived arch-backed into the sea.

Across the Mediterranean came Caesar and ships,
His spikes and axes multiplying the sun,
His sails full silver;
Our sheets still warm and wrinkled,
Cleopatra pretending to sleep,
Antony still naked beneath his armor.

ENOBARBUS PLANS FOR CLEOPATRA

I'll fatten her on steamy mutton cooked in peasant wine
Of the Chianti hills, no alabaster Eros
Born with unnatural perfections will be our God,
But clay household Gods that break in a season,
Found easily as trees in an orchard, that bend
With the wind and bear a fruit luscious and similar.
I'll make her a common soldier's wife with work
In front of the house; I'll couch her on a hard bed
Let her make mystery with straw under her back.
Naked Cleopatra cries. Let there be no more vanities.
I offer water in a pail for a mirror, my promise
To guard in the night against thieves and barbarians.
I am a soldier, will not give up my sword to mystery.
But penny honest, when Antony touches her shoulder
I feel useless flesh about my face, a failure
My body separates from itself, like a beaten army
Whose privates hardly follow my hoarse commands;
My hands are smeared with cold and freckles.
I who took girls to Rome, virgins to the sea,
Know this was not soldiery, but a boy's pluck,
I cannot go to battle hoping Cleopatra watches,
If she looks past me I have no retreats or parries.
Great Eros, I wait beside her
To hand her a glass if she will drink.

CHARMIAN TO ENOBARBUS

I have watched my queen's tricks and when the feasts are over
I eat from plate to plate and have my fill
Of chicken and melon kings and princes did not touch,
Sword buckling and unbuckling in her chamber.
Once Caesar in his prime arrived unexpected,
Cleopatra off on a journey, his hottest lust
Fresh from fighting his death he gave to me.
Love's music is the trumpet and the harp.
Notice she moves her hand like the Nile: a trick.
You think that majesty is closeness to the Gods?
Cleopatra learns from tides and they from her.
Heavy Enobarbus, I like your weight,
I'll hold your head in my lap as she holds Antony's,
No closer can you come to her. Sail here,
I'll wash the honey from our sheets in the Nile.

FULVIA TO CLEOPATRA: A FIRST WIFE'S COMPLAINT

I fixed my house grandest on the Aventine,
Detailed with flowers, choice rugs and gold lamps;
Love's filament that held for twenty years
Snapped in Egypt's darkness.
Queen of whores,
A rhinoceros horn thrust between your thighs
Would wear to dust in a single evening
Before the rising cocks crow your credits,
And morning drives you to pasture.

Great Rome in need of heroes
Eyed its triumphant soldiers,
Its wharfs for sailors,
Found Mark Antony swaggering along the Tiber.
He came to me
Through the triumphant arched legs of pansies.
They wooed him to the Forum, kissed him
Into war; took advantage of the lonely field,
He gained rank, by turning flank.
Those were his whistling days,
Under the arches, flowers and washlines.
I arranged our meetings near the Temple of Mars,
Boasted my father's lands and ships sacked
At Carthage, begot his proposal
Which I read in my garden on a marble chair
Carved with a single lion, in lovely, lonely May.
We married in the temple: my wedding guests roared
To the baths of Caesar following my groom.
He came to me almost useless, a colt
With a soft bottom, wanting to be mounted.
I just took him to the fields,
Let him idle swordless in the sun,
Watching the hawks attack.

That night Antony conquered all my towns.
My walls are leveled, my roofs are charred,
O Cleopatra, think what he shall do to your kingdom.

MENAS:	These three world sharers, these competitors,
	Are in thy vessell. Let me cut the cable.
	And when we are put off, fall to their throats.
	All there is thine.
POMPEY:	Ah, this thou should'st have done
	And not spoken on't! In me, 'tis villainy;
	In thee, it had been good service.

ANOTHER REPLY FOR POMPEY

Cut the cable. But not their throats. Caesar
Antony and Lepidus are in my sack.
Below common skies, ordinary winds
Sail my miraculous cargo past the Gods.

The world, my world, wherever an eye can see,
Notices no change. Rome, Neptune, Venus,
Keep divinity, I mortality,
The rudder doesn't budge, my oars chained to kings
Rise and fall as Gods, break their locks.
My galley slave brain holds fast, O Gods let me
Pace beyond my nature, for I am not natural,
On my oar's chain and on my deck I carve
I am not Caesar's.

Caesar snores, Antony sleeps, Lepidus dreams.
The tides and populations follow these moons.
Had I been born to this as Caesar, my dreams
Would be natural; these calm sleepers slept,
Could wake the people, as wolf bitches wake
Their blind young. Cut their imperial throats!
Let the wind pipe through Caesar back to Rome.
Cut their throats! Invited guests,
Given such brief hospitality,
Such poor fare on my ship, as on the earth;
Romans, even the Gods murder all their guests.

RETURN TO ROME

Today in Rome, heading down
Michelangelo's *Spanish Steps*,
under an unchanging moon,
I held on to the balustrade,
grateful for his giving me a hand.
All for love, I stumbled over the past
as if it were my own feet. Here, in my twenties,
I was lost in love and poetry. Along the Tiber,
I made up Cubist Shakespearean games.
(In writing, even in those days,
I cannot say it was popular to have "subjects"
any more than painters used sitters. But I did.)
I played with an ignorant mirror for an audience:
my self, embroiled with personae
from *Antony and Cleopatra*. Delusions of grandeur!
They were for a time my foul-weather friends—
as once I played with soldiers
on the mountainous countryside of a purple blanket.

2002

SIGN ON THE ROAD

1.

The Atlantic a mile away is flat.
I rent this summer in Amagansett;
I see bayberries and pines. A one-eyed hound
Visits. Nothing is very far from the ground,
This is potato country, yellow and white
Blossom barely. Above the gravel pit
It is hardly wild. I find a snake skin
Pressed into the asphalt. I use tin
Roofing to scrape it up, and throw deep
Into a field the pearl leather. I keep
The tin to paint my sign MOSS in red,
Lean it on a fence where worms have fed;
I make my own target, throw my stone,
I nail my name down into my bone,
It falls in the grass, I pick it up again
Like a sock-apple sweetened in the ditch.
I hope my sign will stand against the pitch
Of summer rain; crash in Atlantic hurricanes,
Drumming my name that creaks and grinds,
"Who am I to think," above the torn-out roots,
On a piece of tin colder than the wind.

2.

My friends, Moss is on the fence in Long Island,
The sea, a distance away like a grandfather
At a family reunion, says it's all sand.
But Moss is on the fence; it might as well

Be charged with high voltage, or painted blue
For all the good that will come of that.
It is a fact and if I scrape my name off
With a knife, the wood is wet underneath,
Just as sand is moist when you kick it up.
I suppose something like this wetnesss and the sun
Made the first living thing, the first sub-roach
That danced its way from under dead matter.
In the beginning before darkness was there a death?
Of course the wind or a telephone call
Moves the earth a little. Damn little.
The apple falls like an apple, and leaves
Hit the earth in their leafy way, and Moss
Shall be no exception. One fine day
I shall fall down like myself in a prison of anger.
Any day is a good day to be born.
I obey the orders of trees.
Moss is on the fence in Amagansett.

PLUMAGE

Off Montauk highway I watch a swan
Clam-gray in the remnant marsh, surrounded
By yesterday's swollen bread; jabbed, he attacks
The stick, and an old automobile tire,
Like great adversaries—moves out of reach,
Trumpeting at the stone-throwing rabble.

Those ancient kisses, those first days were best,
My flesh in cloud almost moved the world.
Was there ever a love more pompous, more foolish?
For fifteen years my mind: a bird that would
Not fly south—something like a swan circling
One place, refusing shelter.

I stand in the reeds under faded cloud.
All that plumage, the pomp of generations
In my wings, push back the mob:
The mercenary cold, the perjuring snows.
Lady, this summer when the world beckons
I shall follow, next winter I go South.

THE GENTLE THINGS

I have had enough of Gods
And disaster;
The gentle things,
All loved ones survive,
Water survives in water,
Love in love.

I lie! The dead stain
Only themselves,
The wolf tears at the world,
Says, *nothing is:*
And the wolf is not the wind,
Is death's fingernail.

Dampness to dampness,
Had I been given
Only life's issue,
Not the song, or the silence
After the singing,
I should be content.

RETURN FROM SELLING

I comply with these disorders to give myself
a wanderer's hope of inn or friendship;
I exchange the day for a room, the room for night,
and briefest thoughts of people still aloof,
common among these city rooms as sleep.
Like a starfish out of its element,
I pick up a book after a long, almost wasted day—
I am back in Athens.
When I was a boy I was carried on my father's shoulders
to Athens, Istanbul and Cairo, I disappeared
for awhile in the red-light district of Algiers.
I was cuddled by laughing, auburn-haired women
who kissed me for nothing.
I look forward to the wall, back to my mind's wall,
a corrupt kingdom. I am an idle craftsman,
shouting and selling at the gate. In the dark,
my mind keeps back neither the ooze of Africa,
nor the Arctic's superfluous snow,
nor will I be made traitor to love's loyalty
by the empty bed that informs against me,
nor will I forget the angel smiling in the doorknob.

FOR DOCTOR GRUBIN

I have a Baroque painting, an execution—
a martyr, Saint Simon, is being sawed
in half by two soldiers. The saw does not cut
the man clean down the middle but bends
around the bone obstructions.
The painting disgusts my uncle, a doctor.
"Why glorify death?" he asks. "Isn't there enough
death in the world." I answer lamely,
"But it is a beautiful painting."
I've been told—when I was a year or two,
when I was thrown down hard on the bed,
my tongue was cut in two, it was
my uncle's advice not to touch it,
not to stitch it up. He left my tongue
dangling, bleeding disgustingly.
He saved my speech—
or was it that about the same age,
on walks with my father
I heard Shakespeare above my head.

TWO FISHERMEN

My father made a synagogue of a boat.
I fish in ghettos, cast toward the lilypads,
strike rock and roil the unworried waters;
I in my father's image: rusty and off hinge,
the fishing box between us like a covenant.
I reel in, the old lure bangs against the boat.
As the sun shines I take his word for everything.
My father snarls his line, spends half an hour
unsnarling mine. Eel, sunfish and bullhead
are not for me. At seven I cut my name for bait.
The worm gnawed toward the mouth of my name.
"Why are the words for temple and school
the same?" I asked, "And why a school of fish?"
My father does not answer. On a bad cast
my fish strikes, breaks water, takes the line.

Into a world of good and evil, I reel
a creature languished in the flood. I tear out
the lure, hooks cold. I catch myself,
two hooks through the hand,
blood on the floor of the synagogue. The wound
is purple, shows a mouth of white birds;
hook and gut dangle like a rosary,
another religion in my hand.
I'm ashamed of this image of crucifixion.
A Jew's image is a reading man.
My father tears out the hooks, returns to his book,
a nineteenth-century history of France.
Our war is over:
death hooks the corner of his lips.
The wrong angel takes over the lesson.

THE RED FIELDS

Should anyone care, I love those red fields
of poppies growing under the wheat,
the Mediterranean to the south
blue to the end of the world, blue as—
I think of eyes, silk dresses, cornflowers,
I'm lousy on blue, but when I think of red
I know I may be talking about the sublime:
say, these red fields, or poppies in the snow
caught in a mountain's throat,
or the loner near the railroad track in Long Island,
coming out of nowhere.
I've seen ten miles of poppies in a storm—
like a child peeking between the legs of his mother—
an ocean of blood I crossed
dragged by a team of mysterious horses.

SQUALL

I have not used my darkness well,
nor the Baroque arm that hangs from my shoulder,
nor the Baroque arm of my chair.
The rain moves out in a dark schedule.
Let the wind marry. I know the creation
continues through love. The rain's a wife.
I cannot sleep or lie awake. Looking
at the dead I turn back, fling
my hat into their grandstands for relief.
How goes a life? Something like the ocean
building dead coral.

WEDDING INVITATION

I leap high as I can for joy, higher than you think I can.
My son writes he is marrying in September in Fiesole,
I leap over my dogs, whom he invited,
although they don't understand weddings.
You, dear reader, are also invited, after all the funerals I brought you to.
I've always been a drum major for a brass band called hope—
even when the band wasn't there. I suggest to my son
he ready his foot to break the wine glass in a white cloth
in memory of the destruction of the Temple. If he doesn't care to,
I'll leave the wine glass in white cloth around, so it may break
by happy accident. I never broke a wine glass
except when it fell off the table, or in rage. My best advice:
the usual public vows are not for nothing, when there's a problem
talk it over. I hope family history does not weigh heavier than
love and honorable intention. Bless you both,
now let the centaurs and Russian dancers in.

2003

GOD POEM

1.

Especially he loves
his space and the parochial darkness.
They are his family, from them grow his kind:
idols with many arms and suns that fathered
the earth, among his many mirrors, and some
that do not break:
rain kept sacred by faithful summer grasses,
fat Buddha and lean Christ, bull and ram,
horns thrusting up his temple and cathedral—
mirrors, but he is beyond such vanities.
Easy to outlive
the moment's death having him on your knees—
grunting and warm he prefers wild positions:
he mouths the moon and sun, brings his body
into insects that receive him beneath stone,
into fish that leap as he chases,
or silent stones that receive his silence.
Chivalrous and polite, the dead take
his caress, and the sea rolling under him
takes his fish as payment and his heaps of shells.

2.

As he will,
he throws the wind arch-backed on the highway,
lures the cat into moonlit alleys,
mountains and fields with wild strawberries.
He is animal,

his tail drags uncomfortably, he trifles
with the suck of bees and lovers, so simple
with commonplace tongues—his eyes ripple
melancholy iron and carefree tin,
his thighs are raw from rubbing,
cruel as pine, he can wing an eagle off a hare's spine,
crouch with the Sphinx, push bishops down
in chilly chapels, a wafer in their mouths,
old men cry out his passage through their bowels.

3.

No word, none of these, no name, "Red Worm! Snake!"
What name makes him leave his hiding place?
Out of the null and void,
no name and no meaning: God, Yahweh, the Lord,
not to be spoken to, he never said a word
or took the power of death: the inconspicuous
plunge from air into sea he gave to us,
winds that wear away our towns . . . Who breathes
comes to nothing: absence, his caress, a world.

INDEX OF TITLES AND FIRST LINES

224

E

F

G

H

I

226

M

N

O

229

230

ABOUT THE AUTHOR

Stanley Moss was born in New York City. He was educated at Trinity College and Yale University. He makes his living as a private art dealer, largely in Spanish and Italian old masters, and is the publisher and editor of The Sheep Meadow Press, a non-profit press devoted to poetry.